Bike-Tripping

Coast to Coast

Bike-Tripping
Coast to Coast

Anita Notdurft-Hopkins

cbi Contemporary Books, Inc.
Chicago

Library of Congress Cataloging in Publication Data

Notdurft-Hopkins, Anita.
  Bike-tripping coast to coast.

  Includes index.
  1. Cycling—United States.   2. Bicycles and
tricycles. I. Title.
GV1045.N67 1978 796.6'0973 77-91185
ISBN 0-8092-7687-9
ISBN 0-8092-7686-0 pbk.

To my husband, Philip

Copyright © 1978 by Anita Notdurft-Hopkins
All rights reserved
Published by Contemporary Books, Inc.
180 North Michigan Avenue, Chicago, Illinois 60601
Manufactured in the United States of America
Library of Congress Catalog Card Number: 77-91185
International Standard Book Number: 0-8092-7687-9 (cloth)
                                    0-8092-7686-0 (paper)

Published simultaneously in Canada by
Beaverbooks
953 Dillingham Road
Pickering, Ontario LlW 1Z7
Canada

Contents

Introduction

Finding the Sanity Machine

In a world seemingly gone mad with mechanization, and where the dollar seems to be all important, there is a growing need to seek out places that are far away from the noise and confusion, to find activities that are physically and mentally stimulating, and to pursue a form of recreation that is done for sheer pleasure and renewal of the spirit. For many, this road to happier times can begin on a bicycle.

Bicycling and the constant delight and enjoyment that come from it may be the best way to restore some peace to your world. The bicycle can become your time machine, slowing down the passing scene to one of comprehension and unity. The pedal rhythm is your mantra, freeing your mind to another level of awareness. By the strength of a body made stronger in spite of yourself, you begin, perhaps, to understand the mysterious rhythms of nature, to understand and experience that other world that is out there somewhere beyond the city sprawl.

This is what this book is about — to help you find the sanity machine so that you can discover that other world. It is also about the longest continuous bicycle trail in the world — the Trans-America — which was inaugurated during the bicentennial year by several thousand bicyclists from the United States and other countries around the world. The touring information in this book is related specifically to this trail. However, that does not mean you cannot tour elsewhere. You can and you should. Since the Trans-America Trail covers all riding challenges, you should be able to apply any information relative to one area to another area of similar terrain and weather, and therefore, you should be able to tour anywhere else quite successfully, pleasantly, and well prepared.

I toured the Trail in the bicentennial year of 1976, sometimes riding independently and sometimes leading groups of other cyclists. (I had taken part in and passed the Bikecentennial leadership training school.)

America is a vast land of many faces, and the Trans-America Trail is beckoning you to come chase your gypsy spirit across its quiet frontiers, away from the busy ciy in a way that is leisurely, unpolluting, and healthful. You can

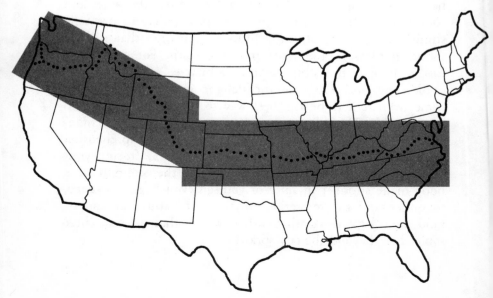

travel through green countryside alive with bird songs, over windblown desert and towering, unexplored mountains, past white frame towns which have changed little since the Conestogas first stopped there. You can discover for yourself that part of your land for what it used to be and still is. Somewhere out there is beauty, love, and kindness. I know because I found it many times on the Trans-America Trail.

Anyone who seriously begins to contemplate bicycle touring can no longer be considered a beginner. Yet, almost without exception, every bicycle book ever written is for the beginner. Where do the more advanced riders turn when they want to find out more than the basics? This book has been written exclusively and specifically for the person who wants to begin touring, whether it be for a 50-mile weekend or a 4,300-mile summer.

It is with this person in mind that I have used terms and expressions without feeling it necessary to define them. If some of the terms do happen to be unfamiliar to you, simply refresh your memory by reading any one of the many more basic books.

In writing a book of this nature, there are two ways something can be stated. I have tried, as much as possible, to stay within the realm of factual information. But quite often it is easy to drop over into the never-never land of theory and opinion. In fact, many statements accepted and repeated by the "experts" are nothing more than theory or opinion. There is nothing wrong with theory or opinion, especially if it works to one's satisfaction. As long as one is not confused with fact, there should be no problems. The reader should be able to tell with little difficulty when I switch to personal opinion. Bike recommendations and brand name accessories are within this category. I mention those brands which, from my personal experience, are trouble free. Each rider is free to pick and choose. Others will recommend with equal conviction brands not mentioned within these covers. The brands I mention are among the best currently available. They are dependable and they will give you a basis for com-

parison in your own selection. After all, you want components which will carry you across America. *Anything* will
work long enough to get you around the block.

Much tour information is available directly from Bikecentennial. Without duplicating their written effort, I have tried
to cover some additional questions and to expand upon their
material. And in the process, the reader will find interwoven
the philosophical thoughts of my 4,300-mile summer.

At the end of this book are a list of names and addresses
for additional information, a few recommended book titles,
and camping and bicycle catalog supply houses which carry
complete lines of touring equipment.

There are several people to whom credit should go for their
help in this endeavor: Jay Anderson, and the trustees of Bryn
Mawr College, Dave E. Brown, Linda Robbins, Lloyd Sumner
— who circumnavigated the globe and is writing a book to be
published in 1978 — Billy Stewart IV, and Marshall Strickler
who allowed me to use some of their journal notes; Matthew
Cohn from Bikecentennial who supplied me with names, addresses, and reams of miscellaneous information; to Bikecentennial for the use of their wealth of material; and to Leon Taylor
who critiqued the manuscript for technical accuracy.

part 1
Preparing for the Big Tour

What Is a Touring Bicycle?

Having the right equipment will make your touring days so much easier. With it, you can become a relaxed, confident rider and enjoy anxiety-free days. It is no fun to have something major break down or to discover 300 miles from nowhere that the equipment you have is all wrong. And believe me, there are some stretches in the western half of the Trans-America Trail that are that desolate. Yet everyone knows someone who rode around the world on a $60 dime store special. This is the exception, not the rule, and sheer luck. So, too, the rider with $1,000 Golden Glitter is another exception. Somewhere between these two extremes exists the happy medium.

Frame

Nothing on your bicycle is more important than the frame (see Figure 1.1). If you buy a cheap frame (read frame as bicycle), you will find it is quite often out of alignment and is made of heavy tubing reminiscent of water pipes. This type of cheap frame usually is difficult to balance, is dangerous on fast down-hills, and requires too much of your energy just to drive it for-ward — a real energy waster.

Price Comparisons

You should get as good a frame (bike) as you can afford, of course. At today's inflated prices the starting point is some-where around $200, depending upon brand names and/or the bike's standard components. That may sound like a lot, but a good bike will last indefinitely. And if you are going to put close to 5,000 miles on it in just one summer, which is what you will do if you ride the entire Trans-America Trail, you are getting by cheaply. You would spend almost that much for gasoline alone if you drove a car that same distance; or figured at today's opera-ting cost of 15ᶜ per mile, it would cost $750.

Of course, you can also spend more than $200, but this is not necessary. You can certainly spend less, but I would not recom-mend it. Since the bike boom began, a lot of junk has flooded the market. Everyone wants to make a buck. There is also a good side to the bike's increased popularity in that the top manufac-turers have upgraded their lines because of that same demand. Prices, too, on top line components are becoming very com-petitive as bikers become more sophisticated.

If you shop around and compare the many different bicycles within the $200 price range, you will find all have about the same top line components, usually Japanese: cotterless cranks, alloy rims, Weinmann or dia Compe center pull brakes, and case-hardened bearing surfaces. Look also for such extras as fin-gertip shifters, rat trap pedals, toe clips, alloy rims, and high pressure gum wall tires.

Slightly below this price range the biggest difference in qual-ity will be found in areas you cannot see — the bearing race sur-faces — even though the components quite often will be the same brand. If you look closer, you will find that brands such as

Sun Tour and Shimano have three, four, five, and even six grades of derailleurs, for example. There is such a thing as bottom of the line even with top quality manufacturers. These should be avoided when you are building a touring bicycle. But let's get back to the unseen area. In the cheaper products, instead of machined case-hardened bearing surfaces throughout the hubs, cranks, and headset, there are cheap stamped rings. These are nothing more than dished washers which are softer than the bearings. As you ride, the bearings will gradually wear a groove into this ring which, as the groove becomes deeper, increases the wear of the ball bearings; this increases the rolling resistance and friction.

In top line components, however, the machined case-hardened bearing surfaces are harder than the steel ball bearing, and as you ride each surface polishes the other. The mirror-like surface that results as you add up the miles makes a slicker running, smoother hub, crank, and headset.

The frame (read frame) will always be better in the $200 bike. Quite often the three main tubes — top, seat, and down tube — are made with Reynolds 531 or Chrome Molybdenum. It is also rare to find frames within this price range which are out of alignment.

Dimensions and Stiffness

Manufacturers have their own characteristic frame dimensions and degrees of stiffness. What a tourer needs is not found in the sharp-angled track bike nor in most road racing frames, the head tube and seat tube angles of which are often 74 or even 75 degrees. The touring frame should be 72 or 73 degrees. Reputable bike dealers should be able to tell you what the degrees are on a particular bike. This angle plus the fork rake will then determine the other dimensions. Fork rake should be not more than 2½ inches and not less than 2 inches. If it is too long, the bike will not corner well; too steep, and it responds too easily which is fine for road racers, but not tourers.

The chain stay should be at least 16½ inches long. If it is not, you could never have a 15-speed gear system because chain deflection would be too great. For that matter, even a 10-speed system with the extremely low gears and wide ranges would be difficult to manage.

The wheelbase should be at least 41 to 43 inches long. The various angles, fork rake, and chain stay length will determine this measurement. The longer the wheelbase, the easier it is to control the load you will carry.

Ideally, a frame should be stiff enough to transmit all energy to the rear wheels, and yet flexible enough to absorb all road shocks. Thus, the touring frame, under normal riding weight conditions, will have a 72 degree head and seat angle, a two inch fork rake, and 17 inch chain stays. This frame is comfortable, but it is not exceptionally responsive as is the road racer. It is easy to ride and will carry the load adequately.

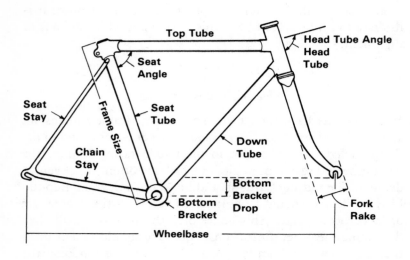

FIGURE 1.1   Ten-Speed Frame

Finally, and equally important, is the stiffness of the frame or the degree of flex in the machine. When you put 20 to 40 pounds or more of dead weight on that frame, you do not want one so flexible that it shakes on fast downhills and swings with every pedal revolution. The only real way to tell is to ride the bike far enough to get the feel of it. Unfortunately, that usually is not possible when buying a new bike from a dealer. You will have to base your decision on what others tell you, which quite often is not as factual as it is opinionated. Besides, how stiff is stiff? A frame can be so stiff as to be lifeless and tiring to ride because every road shock is telegraphed up to you. I can say on good authority and personal experience that Motobecane and Azuki both make ideal touring frames in the $200 and up price range. There are a number of other brands, but these two will give you a starting point.

Throughout this discussion, the diamond style frame is the one referred to, or if you prefer, the man's frame. In fact, the drop frame (the girl's frame) should not even be considered for touring, as by its very nature, it is a much weaker frame. Most flex travels up the seat tube, and if the support tube (top tube) which is nonexistent on this style is only six to nine inches above the pedals, a lot of seat tube remains unsupported. If you get the right size frame in the first place, you have nothing to fear about falling on the top tube.

The mixte would be a good compromise when the diamond frame is out of the question. It is much stronger than the drop frame, but not quite as strong as the pure diamond. Anyone who is serious about cycling — man or woman — should choose a bike on the basis of quality and design rather than anatomy.

Wheels play a determining part in overall bicycle stiffness. Keep this in mind when comparing frame stiffness. If the wheel consists of a low flange hub and a four cross spoke lacing pattern, it will be more flexible than a wheel made with a high flange hub and a three cross spoke lacing pattern. The explanations and specifics of wheels will follow later in this chapter, but for now let's accept this last sentence as a truth and see how this affects the bicycle's performance. Many manufacturers soften a

very stiff frame with the low flange hub, especially in the
cheaper models. Take notice of this. Such practice simply adds
more confusion when you are trying to determine frame stiffness. The most energy-wasting combination would be a flexible
frame with this wheel and yet, this ridiculous idea actually finds
its way to the marketplace in some bikes.

For most touring situations, the ideal combination is a stiff,
but lively, frame with wheels of a high flange hub and a three
cross spoke lacing. But, you are thinking, racers use low flange
hubs and, therefore they must be better. Not so. The reason you
see racing bikes with low flange hubs is because the steep angles
(74 degree plus) found on racing frames and forks make for a
very stiff, rigid frame. They have that type of frame, not so
much for stiffness, but for fast, tight turns and hairline control.
The low flange hubs soften the ride. It is as simple as that. Low
flange hubs weigh slightly less, but that consideration is secondary to the softer riding wheel.

Size and Comfort

After you have found the bicycle of your dreams, be sure to get
the right size. Most production made bikes have 19-, 21-, 23-, or
25-inch frames. This is not to be confused with wheel size. All
good 10-speeds have 27-inch wheels. Frame size numbers refer
to the height of the seat tube. If you straddle the top tube and
stand flat in the same type of shoe you will wear when riding,
there should be one inch of space between the top tube and
your anatomy. Let's suppose you have tried a 23-inch frame on
for size and find there is less than a half inch space. In theory
that frame still fits, just barely, and the 21-inch frame would be,
in this same instance, slightly too small. You should take the
21-inch frame although the difference is more than one inch.
You will be getting a lighter bike because of the smaller frame.
This may seem contrary to your sense of getting your money's
worth, but why opt for the heavier bike when the idea is lightness? You should also forget about whatever ego satisfaction
there may be to having the bigger bike.

Body comfort is more important than ego satisfaction any day. Since the seat tube is slightly shorter so are the top tubes, and obviously all the other dimensions will vary somewhat according to size. Frame builders quite often make the top tube much longer than what is actually needed. So beware of the long top tubes. They are fine for racers who want that ultra low profile. However, tourers ride more erect, because it is more comfortable, and so the shorter top tube found on the smaller frame choice is just ideal. This is why the seat height is adjustable and different lengths of handlebar stems are made, ranging from no extension at all to an extension of as much as six inches. You can always change the length of the handlebar stem to fit your own arm length. But if the top tube is already so long as to be uncomfortable, and you have the shortest handlebar extension, there is nothing more you can do with it. This bicycle is not the right design for you.

If you believe your present frame is a little large, there is a simple trick which will help solve your problem. Lower the wheel size from 27 inches to 26 inches. The smaller diameter will obviously lower the top tube by one half inch; and that is a lot less expensive than replacing the entire bicycle. Remember though, that you changed your gear ratios, and you will have to refer to a gear chart for 26-inch wheels to recalibrate them (see Chapter 2).

Today's frames are made out of a number of materials, the most popular being Reynolds 531 (pronounced five-three-one), which can be straight gauge or the better quality known as double butted. There are also Super Vitus and Chrome-Molybdenum — both equally as good as Reynolds. For the ultra expensive frame material, there is titanium. And the newest, carbon fiber, a very rigid frame material, is not recommended for the touring bicycle at this time. For the frame alone, when made of carbon fiber, you will spend about $750.

Wheels

Next to the frame in bicycle importance are the wheels. In fact, many custom frame builders consider the wheels as a part of the total frame design rather than a separate component.

Types

How and where you plan to ride will determine the type of wheel needed. Earlier I said that the ideal touring wheel is a high flange hub with a three cross spoke lacing pattern. For the purpose of clarity, let's look at the difference between the more popular types of wheels. There are the two basic hub sizes. The high flange has a diameter usually between 65–69mm, while the better quality low flange or small flange hubs have a diameter between 40–44mm. This means that the smaller the flange, the longer the spoke required, and the longer the spoke, the more flexible the wheel. The number of spokes that each spoke crosses will further determine the final spoke length and wheel flex. A spoke that crosses only two other spokes is shorter than the spoke that crosses three or four other spokes. With that piece of information, you now can understand how a shorter two cross spoke lacing pattern on a low flange hub would make a stiffer wheel than the low flange hub laced with a four cross pattern.

The same thing applies to high flange hubs. However, the same cross pattern will be stiffer with the high flange hub because the spokes are always shorter.

If you are going to be doing a great deal of rough-road or off-the-road riding, the low flange hub and the three or four cross lacing pattern is the best. Otherwise, you should stick with the high flange hub.

One last piece of information before we go into the specific touring wheel. Most hubs come with 36 spoke holes. Sometimes a person will find hubs and rims with 40 spokes or even 32. The number of spokes does not affect the flex or stiffness of the wheel, but only the strength of the wheel and its ability to carry a heavy load. Occasionally, a tourer will decide to use a 40-spoke hub and rim for that reason; but it is not necessary unless your weight is above average and you are carrying everything you own. Even then the 40-spoke hub is usually used only on the rear wheel where the greater percentage of concentrated weight is. This is done to ward off spoke breakage.

The Touring Wheel

The interesting thing about wheels and spokes is that you will almost never break a spoke on the front wheel while riding. All spokes will eventually break, and, given enough time, you will break spokes, but generally on the rear wheel and almost always on the freewheel side. The main reason for this is that the freewheel side is under constant torque created between the front and rear gear and chain drive train. The twisting of the spokes is even greater when you use the low gears found on most touring bikes, and in time they will snap like a wire that has been flexed once too often.

For that reason, you should never go on a tour without two things: additional spokes the right length for your wheel and a freewheel remover. This means you will have to know the make of your freewheel before you can buy the right remover. There are many different freewheels on the market. If you are wondering why you need to remove the freewheel just to be able to replace a spoke, one glance at your wheel should answer that question. (The technique of replacing a spoke is covered in Chapter 13.)

The front wheel is not much of a problem. A high flange hub and a three cross spoke lacing pattern, and you can almost forget about it. But the rear wheel is something else. Not only must it hold up under the load and torque, but it must also hold up under one other unique thing called the dish. If you examine the width of your rear hub, you will discover that it is narrower than the front hub. The reason is so that the freewheel width can be accommodated within that axle. The rear tire is centered over the axle and not the hub by dishing the wheel. It is flatter on the freewheel side, which means that all the spokes on that side are made slightly shorter in order to pull the wheel over to that side. Remember, the shorter the spoke, the less flexible it is. It is interesting to note that where you would want flex to take up some of the torque, just the opposite is happening. But there is a wheel trick coming your way. If you know how to lace wheels and have a wheel trueing stand at your disposal or know someone who specializes in wheel building who can do this for you, you can lace the rear wheel into a three cross on the left side and a four cross on the freewheel side. What was that? you say. It does work. You will need three different spoke lengths to accomplish this, but by crossing four spokes on the freewheel side you are compensating for the torque by using a longer spoke and hence more flex on that side. Yet, the wheel acts just like a three cross as far as total stiffness is concerned. This seems to cut down the number of broken spokes.

New Lightweight Tires

In the past year several tire manufacturers have introduced a super lightweight and strong clincher tire. These new clinchers compete with the sew-ups for lightness. Michelan and Cycle Pro each have clinchers which weigh only five grams more than a sew-up (28 grams equal one ounce). You will get a flat tire eventually, regardless of the kind of tire you have, but clinchers are easier to repair. With practice, clinchers are as fast to change on the road as sew-ups, and there is no glue to fool with. Clinchers are cheaper and tougher over rocky roads, too.

With clinchers available, there is no reason for tourists to bother with sew-ups again. And they are a bother! (Of course, there are those who will take exception to this.) Sew-ups do not hold up over gravel roads; they are very expensive (one brand recommended for tourists costs $30.00 each), take unlimited patience to repair, and are not even stocked in many of the smaller bike shops. Sew-ups are great for the big weekend club race, but other than that forget them.

In 1976 I rode the entire Trans-America Trail with Schwinn Letour, neither the lightest tire nor one of those new lightweights, but a highly recommended touring tire, and I did not have one flat! That was an exception, but it *is* a good tire. This year I have the new lightweight Cycle Pro 270's, and so far I have had no trouble with them.

You will need narrower rims to go along with these narrow lightweights. Araya alloy is one which is 1-1/8 inch wide. For the discerning cyclist, it is a tire idea worth looking into.

One final word about rims. There are steel rims and alloy rims. Steel rims are not any stronger than alloy if the wheel is laced properly to start. They are heavier, but heavier is not necessarily stronger. Both will bend; but unlike alloy, steel, once bent, cannot be bent back into its original shape without having a weak spot at that point. Alloy will retain its strength because of its molecular structure.

At the beginning of this chapter, I mentioned a suggested price for your touring bicycle. This is taking for granted that you would not purchase this bike in a department store or drug store. Those bikes, in general, are "drugs" on the market. Department stores usually display their bikes in the toy department, which gives you some idea of the level they place their product. You probably could not find a bicycle in those places that sells for much over $100. By all means, you should support your local bicycle dealers. They, at least, have some kind of repair service, which is a consolation should your new dream machine malfunction.

2

Solving the Gear Mystery

At least once during the summer of '76, someone proved that you could ride a single speed coaster brake bike cross country. Okay, so he was the son of Samson or Hercules. However, 99 percent of the bicycles which were seen on the trail that summer were of the ten-speed variety. Common sense will tell you that this is the logical machine for a trip of this nature. Three-speeds and even five-speeds leave much to be desired when touring. At one time the three-speed was high on the list of good quality bicycles, but since the advent of the more popular ten-speed, its quality has gone by the boards. Three-speeds are of little value on the hilly terrain and mountains you will encounter all along the trail — with the exception of the plains of Kansas — because of their limited low gear ratios. Make life easy on yourself and take the ten-speed across the country — ten gears in theory, that is.

Eight Gears on The Ten-Speed

In practice, your ten-speed has only eight usable gears, of which I seldom use more than six. Let me explain. Because of the ex-

FIGURE 2.1 Gear Charts

26" Wheel

Number of teeth, Chainwheel (large front sprocket)

Teeth Per Rear Sprocket	28	32	33	34	36	38	39	40	42	43	44	45	46	47	48	49	50	51	52	53	54	55	56	57	58	59	60	61	62
13	56.0	64.0	66.0	68.0	72.0	76.0	78.0	80.0	84.0	86.0	88.0	90.0	92.0	94.0	96.0	98.0	100.0	102.0	104.0	106.0	108.0	110.0	112.0	114.0	116.0	118.0	120.0	122.0	124.0
14	52.0	59.4	61.2	63.1	66.8	70.5	72.4	74.2	78.0	79.8	81.7	83.5	85.4	87.2	89.1	91.0	92.8	94.7	96.5	98.4	100.2	102.1	104.0	105.8	107.7	109.5	111.4	113.2	115.1
15	48.5	55.4	57.2	58.9	62.4	65.8	67.6	69.3	72.8	74.5	76.2	78.0	79.7	81.4	83.2	84.9	86.6	88.4	90.1	91.8	93.6	95.3	97.0	98.8	100.5	102.2	104.0	105.7	107.4
16	45.5	52.0	53.6	55.2	58.5	61.7	63.3	65.0	68.2	69.8	71.5	73.1	74.7	76.3	78.0	79.6	81.2	82.8	84.5	86.1	87.6	89.3	91.0	92.6	94.2	95.8	97.5	99.1	100.7
17	42.8	48.9	50.4	52.0	55.0	58.1	59.6	61.1	64.3	65.7	67.2	68.8	70.3	71.8	73.4	74.9	76.4	78.0	79.5	81.0	82.5	84.1	85.6	87.1	88.7	90.2	91.7	93.2	94.8
18	40.4	46.2	47.6	49.1	52.0	54.8	56.3	57.7	60.6	62.1	63.5	65.0	66.4	67.8	69.3	70.7	72.2	73.6	75.1	76.5	78.0	79.4	80.8	82.3	83.7	85.2	86.6	88.1	89.5
19	38.3	43.7	45.1	46.5	49.2	52.0	53.3	54.7	57.4	58.8	60.2	61.5	62.9	64.3	65.6	67.0	68.4	69.7	71.1	72.5	73.8	75.2	76.6	78.0	79.3	80.7	82.1	83.4	84.8
20	36.4	41.6	42.9	44.2	46.8	49.4	50.7	52.0	54.6	55.9	57.2	58.5	59.8	61.1	62.4	63.7	65.0	66.3	67.6	68.9	70.2	71.5	72.8	74.1	75.4	76.7	78.0	79.3	80.6
21	35.1	39.6	40.8	42.1	44.6	47.0	48.2	49.5	52.0	53.2	54.4	55.7	56.9	58.1	59.4	60.6	61.9	63.1	64.3	65.6	66.8	68.0	69.3	70.5	71.8	73.0	74.2	75.5	76.6
22	33	37.8	39.0	40.1	42.5	44.9	46.0	47.2	49.6	50.8	52.0	53.1	54.3	55.5	56.7	57.9	59.0	60.2	61.4	62.6	63.8	65.0	66.1	67.3	68.5	69.7	70.9	72.0	73.2
23	31.6	36.1	37.3	38.4	40.7	42.9	44.0	45.2	47.4	48.6	49.7	50.8	52.0	53.1	54.2	55.3	56.5	57.6	58.7	59.9	61.0	62.1	63.3	64.5	65.5	66.6	67.8	68.9	70.0
24	30.3	34.6	35.7	36.8	39.0	41.1	42.2	43.3	45.5	46.5	47.6	48.7	49.8	50.9	52.0	53.0	54.1	55.2	56.3	57.4	58.5	59.5	60.6	61.7	62.8	63.9	65.0	66.0	67.1
25	29.1	33.2	34.3	35.3	37.4	39.5	40.5	41.6	43.6	44.7	45.7	46.8	47.8	48.8	49.9	50.9	52.0	53.0	54.0	55.1	56.1	57.2	58.2	59.3	60.3	61.3	62.4	63.4	64.4
26	28	32.0	33.0	34.0	36	38.0	39.0	40.0	42.0	43.0	44.0	45.0	46.0	47.0	48.0	49.0	50.0	51.0	52.0	53.0	54.0	55.0	56.0	57.0	58.0	59.0	60.0	61.0	62.0
28	26	29.7	30.6	31.5	33.4	35.2	36.2	37.1	39.0	39.9	40.9	41.8	42.7	43.6	44.5	45.5	46.4	47.3	48.2	49.2	50.1	51.0	52.0	52.9	53.8	54.7	55.7	56.6	57.5

FIGURE 2.1 Gear Charts

27" Wheel

Number of teeth, Chainwheel (large front sprocket)

Teeth Per Rear Sprocket	24	26	28	30	32	34	36	38	40	42	44	45	46	47	48	49	50	52	53	54	55	56
12	54.0	58.5	63.0	67.5	72.0	76.5	81.0	85.5	90.0	94.5	99.0	101.2	103.5	105.7	108.0	110.2	112.3	117.0	119.3	121.5	122.7	126.0
13	49.8	54.0	58.1	62.3	66.4	70.6	74.7	78.9	83.1	87.2	91.4	93.4	95.5	97.6	99.7	101.8	103.9	108.0	110.0	112.1	114.2	116.3
14	46.2	50.1	54.0	57.8	61.7	65.5	69.5	73.3	77.1	81.0	84.9	86.7	88.7	90.6	92.6	94.5	96.4	100.3	102.2	104.1	106.0	108.0
15	43.2	46.8	50.4	54.0	57.6	61.1	64.8	68.4	72.0	75.6	79.2	81.0	82.8	84.6	86.4	88.2	90.0	93.6	95.4	97.2	99.0	100.8
16	40.5	43.7	47.2	50.6	54.0	57.2	60.9	64.1	67.5	70.9	74.3	76.0	77.6	79.3	81.0	82.7	84.4	87.8	89.4	91.1	92.8	94.5
17	38.1	41.2	44.4	47.6	50.8	54.0	57.2	60.3	63.5	66.7	69.9	71.5	73.1	74.6	76.2	77.8	79.4	82.6	84.1	85.7	87.3	88.9
18	36.0	39.0	42.0	45.0	48.0	51.0	54.0	57.0	60.0	63.0	66.0	67.5	69.0	70.5	72.0	73.5	75.0	78.0	79.5	81.0	82.5	84.0
19	34.1	36.8	39.7	42.6	45.5	48.2	51.1	54.0	56.8	59.7	62.5	64.0	65.4	66.8	68.2	69.6	71.1	73.9	75.3	76.7	78.1	79.5
20	32.4	35.1	37.8	40.5	43.2	45.9	48.7	51.3	54.0	56.7	59.4	60.8	62.1	63.4	64.8	66.2	67.5	70.2	71.5	72.9	74.5	75.6
21	30.8	33.4	36.0	38.6	41.1	43.7	46.4	48.9	51.4	54.0	56.6	57.9	59.1	60.4	61.7	63.0	64.3	66.9	68.1	69.4	70.7	72.0
22	29.4	31.9	34.3	36.8	39.2	41.6	44.2	46.6	49.1	51.5	54.0	55.2	56.1	57.6	58.9	60.1	61.4	63.8	65.0	66.2	67.5	68.7
23	28.1	30.5	32.8	35.2	37.5	39.9	42.4	44.6	47.0	49.3	51.6	52.8	54.0	55.2	56.3	57.5	58.7	61.0	62.2	63.6	64.5	65.7
24	27.0	29.2	31.5	33.7	36.0	38.2	40.5	42.8	45.0	47.3	49.5	50.7	51.8	52.9	54.0	55.1	56.3	58.6	59.6	60.7	61.8	63.0
25	25.9	28.0	30.2	32.4	34.6	36.7	38.9	41.0	43.2	45.4	47.5	48.6	49.7	50.8	51.8	52.9	54.0	56.2	57.2	58.3	59.4	60.4
26	24.9	27.0	29.0	31.2	33.2	35.3	37.4	39.5	41.5	43.6	45.7	46.7	47.8	48.8	49.9	50.9	51.9	54.0	55.0	56.0	57.1	58.1
27	24.0	26.0	28.0	30.0	32.0	34.0	36.0	38.0	40.0	42.0	44.0	45.0	46.0	47.0	48.0	49.0	50.0	52.0	53.0	54.0	55.0	56.0
28	23.1	25.0	27.0	28.9	30.8	32.8	34.8	36.6	38.6	40.5	42.4	43.4	44.4	45.3	46.3	47.2	48.2	50.1	51.1	52.0	53.0	54.0
29	22.4	24.2	26.1	28.0	29.8	31.6	33.5	35.4	37.2	39.0	41.0	41.9	42.8	43.8	44.7	45.6	46.5	48.4	49.4	50.3	51.2	52.1
30	21.6	23.4	25.2	27.0	28.8	30.6	32.4	34.2	36.0	37.8	39.6	40.5	41.4	42.3	43.2	44.1	45.0	46.8	47.7	48.6	49.5	50.4
31	20.9	22.6	24.4	26.2	27.9	29.6	31.4	33.1	34.8	36.6	38.3	39.2	40.1	41.0	41.8	42.6	43.5	45.2	46.2	47.0	47.9	48.8
32	20.3	22.0	23.6	25.3	27.0	28.7	30.4	32.1	33.7	35.4	37.2	38.0	38.8	39.7	40.5	41.4	42.2	43.9	44.7	45.5	46.4	47.3
33	19.6	21.3	22.9	24.6	26.2	27.8	29.5	31.1	32.7	34.4	36.0	36.8	37.6	38.5	39.3	40.1	40.9	42.6	43.4	44.2	45.0	45.9
34	19.1	20.6	22.2	23.8	25.4	27.0	28.6	30.2	31.8	33.3	35.0	35.7	36.5	37.4	38.1	38.9	39.7	41.3	42.1	42.9	43.6	44.5

treme chain deflection that occurs when you ride on the large rear sprocket and the large front or the small rear sprocket in combination with the small front one, all of the following parts will wear out very fast: the chain, the teeth on these sprockets, and even the derailleur cage if the chain should rub against it. (It invariably will because the chain is running at such a lopsided angle). There is only one combination where the chain is running in a straight line and that is on the large front sprocket and on the middle or third freewheel sprocket.

Another interesting thing about ten-speeds is that you can change the gearing to suit your own personal riding habits. That is why it is important to understand gear charts so that you can equate those figures with your own personal riding strength. By knowing about the various gears available on your bike, you will learn to judge how any given gear will feel.

If you make an effort to comprehend this chapter, you will understand the most important part of your bicycle — and understanding that will greatly aid you in becoming a more efficient cyclist.

Using Gear Charts

Just what do all those figures mean? I prefer to use a gear chart which converts into inches (see Figure 2.1). That means that if you were pedaling a direct drive wheel like your child's tricycle or the old-time ordinaries or penny-farthings, that wheel would be so many inches in diameter. Do not confuse this with circumference. If your front sprocket has 52 teeth and your rear sprocket has 14 teeth, that converts into a 100-inch wheel. That is the same as riding a high wheeler with a big 100-inch-diameter wheel. It would be very hard to ride that up a hill. In fact, to do so with ease, the big wheel would have to be changed to a smaller one, and this would not be practical. However, this is the principle behind shifting your ten-speed. You are actually changing the diameter of that driving wheel. This is a lot easier than having to carry a truckload of different wheel sizes.

To find out what different wheel sizes are on your bike, begin by counting the teeth on all seven sprockets of your ten-speed. Then refer to the chart in Figure 2.1 and you will end up with something that looks like this:

	52	40
14	100.3	—
17	82.6	63.5
21	66.9	51.4
23	61.0	47.0
28	—	38.6

I selected this combination because it is one of the more common combinations from an off-the-shelf bike. As you can readily see by the chart, there is an almost unlimited number of combinations available to you. Two of the spaces are blank because those are the two you should never use.

One of the first things you should notice is that this combination has a 62-inch range (from 100 to 38 = 62). Next is the progression of ratios. There is no duplication of gears although two do come very close — 61 and 63. If you are a strong rider who also travels light, this combination should work well for you even in the mountains. To go higher than 38 inches requires a very strong rider. Most tourists, and certainly most females, will want at least one gear lower than 38 inches. One interesting thing about this combination is the high gear of 100 inches. The only time the average rider would be able to use that gear would be downhill or with a strong tail wind (how often are you blessed with that) or both. In other words, that space could be put to better use with a lower tenth gear. Thus, the following combination is much more practical for the average touring cyclist:

	48	Gear	36	Gear
14	92.6	10	—	9
16	81.0	8	60.9	6
20	64.8	7	48.6	4
23	56.3	5	42.2	2
28	—	3	34.7	1

It still has a wide range, but just by changing both front sprockets and two on the freewheel, the entire range was shifted downward. Again, there is no duplication of any gear, and there is usable spread between them. Several other interesting observations with this combination are as follows: You can still use the lighter, shorter arm rear derailleur. Going smaller in the front, rather than larger in the rear, requires less chain length and trims off some weight, which is the main objective.

Can you begin to see why it is important to know what your gear ratios are? If you do not know how your bike handles in 92.6 or 100.3, for example, then 92.6 will mean nothing to you. If you do know, you can begin to compare one over the other. Somewhere in the potpourri of numbers is the one gear which is the most comfortable of all when you are riding flat and level with little or no wind and your touring packs. Let's assume that it is 64, and you *know* that it is; then that should be your seventh gear, giving you three higher gears and a lot of lower ones.

Look again at our hypothetical gear setup, and this time notice the shifting pattern. To shift consecutively through all the gears requires a lot of back and forth shifting.

Earlier I said that I use only six of the gears on my ten-speed. Let me demonstrate by giving a set of numbers to the front and rear sprockets according to the diagram given in Figure 2.2.

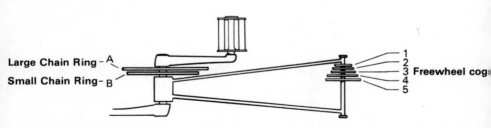

FIGURE 2.2   Drive Train

Begin with the chain on A-1, then A-2, and A-3 (I am shifting into lower gears using only the rear gears). At this point, I shift the front gears to B, the smaller sprocket, and continue B-3, B-4, and B-5. It is smooth and in a direct pattern. Blocked out on the chart, it would look like this:

	48		36	
14	96	A-1		
16	81	A-2	60	B-2
20	64	A-3	48	B-3
23	56	A-4	42	B-4
28			36	B-5

Then there are the other two gears which are surrounded by the broken lines. If you assume that 64 is a little too high and 48 is a little too low, you can always shift up or down to them. You will also notice the range spread within those four gears (64 – 60 – 56 – 48). Regardless of what combination you personally select, you should take all of the above ideas into consideration when working up your touring gears.

I sometimes wonder if it is the macho or the masochist in all of us which causes some riders to have gears which are too high for them. When faced with a hill or mountain pass, they strain, struggle, pant, sweat. For what? They really are not getting up there any faster than they would if they had a lower gear so they could pedal easier and maintain a brisk pedal cadence. (More on that later.) It could be that riders are uninformed. What may have been a comfortable low gear without all that extra baggage is not the right gear now. The lower the gears, the lighter the load seems. Besides, you are not racing, but touring, and you are out there to see something of the countryside. You cannot do that very well if your pulse is pounding against your eardrums. If your gears are suited to you, there should be no reason for pushing your bike up a hill. Walking is just as hard as pedaling or perhaps harder. I have some super low gears on my bike which make riding easier than walking. Whenever you become tired, which all of us do on the real long climbs, you should by all means stop and rest long enough to get your breath, but not so long that your muscles begin to cramp. A minute or two is long enough. Another hint — do not climb hills on a full stomach and avoid soda pop.

"Granny Gears" and the 15-Speed

I like "granny gears" — low gears — when I tour! Let us make another gear chart, only this time let's build a low gear combination. Using the same 48 and 36 sprockets for the front, it would look like the following:

	48	36
14	96	
18	72	54
23	56	42
28	46	34
32		30

Now we have a 66-gear range, but we have created several gaps and no gears in the 60s. We also need what is called a long arm derailleur to handle the wider range. Shimano Crane GS is one of the best with a moderate price tag, and Sun Tour and Campagnolo are two more worth looking into. But we have a 30-inch wheel, and almost everybody will enjoy the hills with this size.

Because of the gaps and other things that are happening here, it brings us to a discussion of the 15-speed. Like the ten-speed, the 15-speed does not have 15 speeds, but only 12 usable gears or twice that of the ten-speed. With these extra six gears, we can fill in the gaps and have a much more even progression of gears.

Time to make another gear chart, and this time it is the one I'd use for cross-country touring. A freewheel cluster of 14 – 18 – 21 – 23 – 28 will work equally as well.

	50	40	34
14	96	77	
18	75	60	
21	64	51	43
28	48	38	32
34		31	27

The gear range is quite wide with a low of 27 inches — or one to one ratio. (If you choose a 32-tooth freewheel cog rather than a 34-tooth, your low will be 28.7 which is still a wall climber.) Another interesting thing is happening with the freewheel. Look at the large seven-tooth jump between the third and fourth freewheel cogs. Yet, by having that third sprocket in the front, this is a workable combination.

For all but the very steepest climbs in the Rockies, the 32-inch gear has been more than adequate. But the Ozarks and the Appalachians are something else, so a 27-inch is kept in reserve just for them.

The front derailleur that I recommend is a Shimano Dura Ace and a Shimano Crane GS on the rear which works like a champ. I also suggest adding the latest in chains, the Shimano Uniglide; you will never miss a gear with this combination. It is very fast and positive.

This freewheel is, as you would imagine, much heavier than the 14 to 28 combination. One way to reduce that weight and still keep the large 34-tooth sprocket is to use the Sun Tour Winner freewheel body, one of the smoothest freewheels on the market. It comes with either steel or alloy cogs. Everybody knows that alloy is much lighter than steel, but for a freewheel part its wear life is very short. However, it is possible to combine the two types, using steel for the smaller and more used cogs and alloy for the 28 and 34, which are the least used.

Hopefuly, the gear mystique is clearer now. After they have made their bikes' gear chart, many riders transfer this information to a small piece of paper which is usually taped to the top of the handlebar stem or the top tube. One glance and you can say to yourself as you pedal along, "I'm in the 64-inch gear."

What makes this information meaningful to you is how each inch gear affects your pedal cadence. You have probably been told that to ride efficiently, your pedal cadence should be somewhere around 70 to 85 rpms. That means at *all* times. Whether you have a flat road, head wind, or a moderate hill, your cadence should be 70 to 85 rpms. Obviously if the gear is too high, you will not be able to turn the pedals that fast, and conversely, if the gear you are in is too low, you will have so little resistance against the pedals that you will spin too fast and waste energy. Knowing when to shift up or down in order to maintain a steady cadence is the major secret of enjoyable, effortless cycling. Accomplish that, and you have at last learned how to make the bicycle do all the work instead of *you.*

3

The All-Important
Remainder

Brakes

The first bicycles did not have brakes. There was no traffic to
contend with, no roads, and riders did not often attempt to
cross mountain passes. Today it is a different story. You either
have workable brakes or risk blowing a tennis shoe at 45 mph.

At present all medium-priced bicycles come with center pull
brakes — usually Weinmann or dia Compe — and a few come
with Universal or Mafac brands on them. These are all good center pulls. Side pull brakes are found only on the cheap bikes or
the very high-class ones. That might not make much sense, but
it is a fact. Campagnolo makes side pull brakes selling for
around $100! Shimano makes some that sell for over $50 which
is still a respectable price tag. How can you have side pulls on a
cheap bike? For one reason, they obviously are made by a lesser
known manufacturer whose complete bikes hardly cost that
much. Second, bottom of the line side pull brakes cost a few

pennies less to manufacture than center pulls, and over the mass production haul the pennies become dollars — simple net profit mathematics.

Cheap center pulls are better than cheap side pulls. For a few cents more, you would do even better to get a decent pair of center pulls. They will require less of your attention and patience to keep them in proper working order.

For the average cyclist, the difference in performance of expensive side pulls — the Campy's or Dura-Ace — is so negligible as to be unnoticeable. It is better to put the $50 to $100 into upgrading the hubs, cranks, or pedals first.

Many of the brake sets include safety brake levers. These are levers which can be reached from the top of the handlebars. They are anything but safe and should be outlawed. First, they are not capable of stopping as efficiently as main levers. To prove that to yourself, compare your stopping power first with one set and then the other. Another more important reason is that when you really must have braking control and balance on rough roads, downgrades, or both, for example, you want to be as low as possible on your bicycle. To use the main levers you must be on the drops of the handlebars, and that naturally puts you into the position of a lower center of gravity. But, you may say, when going downhill I would use the main levers; or on a panic stop I would be able to reach the main levers as quickly. Nonsense! Once you have developed the habit of using those "un-" safety brake levers, you will not think of using the main levers first. And in a panic situation you most certainly will grab the levers that you are most accustomed to using, which in this case are those you should not even have on your bicycle. As for quick accessibility, you have already lost valuable time in braking since these so-called safety levers do not offer much in the way of braking power. Get into the habit of using the main brakes, and you will be a safer rider. By being on the drops, you will at least give yourself a fighting chance.

And, in fact, it was Bikecentennial policy in the summer of 1976 for all group leaders to see to it that these safety levers were removed from all bikes whenever possible.

The remaining bicycle parts are chosen more for personal comfort preferences than for cost versus efficiency. Actually, cost is not even a factor in the following items since it varies only within a few pennies. The following is a list of the items with which I prefer to tour and the reasons why.

The Seat

There are four basic types of seats: (1) the nylon or plastic seat which is sometimes covered with thin layers of leather or plastic; (2) the steel shell covered with padding and usually a plastic layer; (3) the mattress style complete with springs; and (4) the leather seat. I prefer the Brooks or Ideale leather seats and would not use any other style. Leather is like a new shoe, stiff at first, but once it is broken in it becomes your comfortable, priceless old favorite, molded to your anatomy. There are ways to speed up this process such as working Neats foot oil into the underside and using talcum powder and Brooks Proofide leather dressing on the side you sit upon.

Steel should be avoided at all costs! Once that covering is worn off and the so-called padding is pounded down, where are you? Ouch!

Mattress seats are not much better, although they do feel nice and cushy soft at first, and therein lies the problem. They are so cushy you will bounce with every pedal rotation, finally bouncing into a nice set of blisters. Much of the energy you want to travel down your legs to the pedals is absorbed into that seat. Also, they are wider at the front, and for females especially this means the inside of the legs are going to chafe against that part of the seat. If you think that the mattress seat is a girl's seat, think again.

Avocet is the only manufacturer who advertises seats for the female anatomy. They make two styles — a racing and a touring version. The racing models have a softer shell and are more comfortable for shorter rides or weekend riding. The touring model is a higher quality, firmer nylon shell, making it a more efficient and comfortable seat for the long distance touring cyclist. The idea behind the firmer seat is that an experienced cyclist would become uncomfortable from excessive movement caused by too flexible a seat over long distances. (Again — the argument mentioned above against the mattress style seat.) All Avocet seats are available in smooth leather or buffalo covering. The only difference is that buffalo leather does not allow the rider to slip about, and that is just a matter of personal preference.

Another model does come close, not by design, but by accident; it is the Brooks Standard B-15 — a good quality leather seat which is slightly wider across the back.

Shifters

They can be almost anywhere on the frame — the handlebar stem, the down tube, or the top tube. However, if your bike has them on the top tube, I would strongly recommend that you put them somewhere else. If you met some unexpected brick wall, you could land on top of them and injure yourself. My favorite location for shifters is at the end of the handlebars. Commonly called fingertip shifters, they make life much easier when you are riding up Hoosier Pass or through the Ozarks. Here is what happens: when going uphill, the slower you are traveling, the more your balance is affected and the harder it is to remove one or both hands from the handlebars. You will obviously have to do that if your levers are on the down tube. There you are, struggling up this grade, going ever slower. Now you are hanging by your toe clips ready to topple over because you did not dare ride one-handed for the time needed to reach down and shift. All the while you wish the shifters were at your fingertips.

The other beautiful part about fingertip shifters is that to shift into the lower gears on the freewheel, the right-hand (usually) lever is pulled upward, and that is in keeping with your arm's and body's attitude. At the same time, you are also pulling up against your pedal power.

Toe Clips

Neophytes are freaked out by them. Virtuosos swear by them. You should learn to use them. Aside from increasing your pedaling efficiency, they are one of the safest items you could ever hang on your bike. "But," you say, "if I'm going to fall, I don't want to be strapped onto the pedals." And I would reply, "If you are heading for a nasty fall, yes, you do." In a bad fall, you will get abrasions and cuts, but if your legs are flopping around, you stand a good chance of breaking a bone or two. When your foot is held to the pedal, your leg is supported by a steel frame, and you will really have to work at breaking a leg. Toe clips are also nice over a rough road. If your foot is bounced off the pedal, you will lose control of the bike, and you could also get a nasty wallop on the back of your leg with the pedal as it comes around.

There are times when you will want to leave the straps loose, such as in heavy stop-and-go city traffic, a gravel road, or the mountain pass which may slow you to a stop; but in all these cases your feet still will not be bouncing on and off the pedals.

Pages have been written on how to ankle, and you have probably read most of them, so you are familiar with the term and process. If you use toe clips, you will ankle automatically. Without toe clips, ankling is next to impossible. Also, if they are your size (they come in small, medium, large, and extra-large depending upon your shoe size), you will pedal on the ball of your foot without having to think about it.

Another riding technique used with toe clips is spinning — pulling up with one leg while the opposite leg is pushing down. This technique enables you to take the dead weight off the rising pedal and use another set of muscles in the process. Obviously, you cannot pull up without toe clips. About all you can do is take the weight off the pedal. Spinning with toe clips will increase your pedal efficiency at least by 15 percent. And spinning is directly related to cadence. Amazing how it all fits together, isn't it?

Fenders

If you ride a lot in the rain, they are a nice luxury. Simple to install, they keep much of the "gook" off your bike and you do not get the biker's "black back streak." On sunny days though, they are a wind resister of sorts. During the summer of '76, I had fenders and they came in handy for all of four hours. I have since taken them off. This summer when I tour, I will probably have 40 days and 40 nights of rain!

Pannier Racks

Blackburn makes a very stable, extremely lightweight set for front and rear (see Figure 3.1). Kerimore is another brand to look for. Both have more than one point of welded attachment running from the rack to the dropout eyelets. You should look for that in any rack you select. When you have 20 or more pounds hanging from them, you do not want them to start side-swaying as you ride down the road or mountain. Pletcher is fine for carrying a couple of books to the library, but it should be avoided for touring. It has only one point of attachment from rack to frame, and that rod is held to the top of the rack with only a rivet or screw.

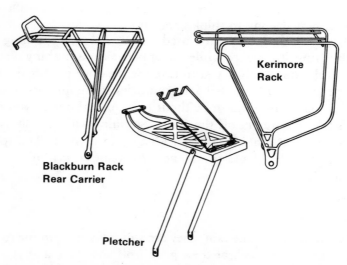

Kerimore
Rack

Blackburn Rack
Rear Carrier

Pletcher

FIGURE 3.1   Types of Pannier Racks

Tire Pumps

Tire pumps are almost as common as weeds and worth about as much. Many of those on the market are made to appeal to children as a novelty item. There are very few which are worth their salt. Racers will tell you about the Silca, which is good but made to fit the presta valve found on sew-up tires. Although presta valves are found on some clincher inner tubes, the more common valve stem is the schrader. Zefal high pressure is a very good tourist pump, and it can be adapted to fit both types of valve stems. It is the easiest hand pump to use because it has a thumb lock which holds the pump on the valve. It also depresses the valve spring so that you do not have to push against that added pressure. This means that with the Zefal, even the weakest individual will be able to put 100 pounds of pressure into the tires.

Water Bottles

Always carry at least one water bottle with you. East of Kansas, towns or houses are usually within a one-bottle distance of water, but in the West you should plan on at least two bottles of water. There are sections in Wyoming and Montana where towns are 50 miles apart or hours away if you are climbing one of the passes on the Continental Divide. You can never have enough water when you are in the middle of nowhere.

Handlebars

There are only two types of handlebars a cyclist-tourist need be aware of — the Maes and Ranndeour styles. Both are of the drop bar configuration. You should not have upright handlebars for long distance riding unless you have a physical problem which demands this style. With drop handlebars, at least six different changes of hand positions are possible. They put your body into a more comfortable position for breathing and weight distribution, and they are safer on downhills and other situations where control and balance are uppermost for safety.

4

Your Pedaled Home

Panniers

Before I go into detail about what items you should consider taking on your trip, let me mention something about panniers — those bicycle suitcases you will be living out of. And living, literally, you will, so getting a good set is a smart investment.

When considering panniers, you should look for a square design rather than a design with triangular or rounded bottoms. Things have a habit of falling to the bottom in those shapes, and nothing stays where you put it. As soon as a "hole" is made by removing something, other things fall into that "hole." Bags with several side pockets are nice, since items can be separated and cataloged.

Attachments

You should stay away from bags with velcrol tabs for rack attachment, because in time, they break down. This is different from velcrol closures which are fine. Metal hooks are the only practical

33

rack attachments. Panniers should fit securely and not shift around on the rack. Designwise, it is important that they not get in your way when you are riding. You should also notice the type of bottom rack attachment. It should be a strong spring and hook combination that fits onto the rack bottom near the frame's dropout eyelets. Make sure that the bag is waterproof and not just water resistant. A bright color like red or better still, yellow, is preferable. Yellow is more visible on overcast and foggy days. The method of hardware attachment to the bag should be checked. Some only have a styrofoam type frame; others have a very lightweight metal frame. Obviously, metal is stronger, and the rivets have less chance of pulling out.

Types

There are many manufacturers of panniers; and just like bike manufacturers, they are out to cash in on the bicycle boom. Very few of them are producing a bag that will stand up over a long trip. If you know that you are going on a short trip — two weeks or less — and it may be the only tour you will ever make, you can get almost anything short of a grocery bag. But if you are going to spend the entire summer on the Trans-America Trail, be smart and get the best you can afford. I have found Kirtland Tour Pacs to be some of the best (see Figure 4.1). Cannondale makes many bags in several price ranges, but their top of the line is almost an exact copy of Kirtland and worth considering for the price difference (see Figure 4.2).

Checklist

Even the very experienced tourist always ends up taking more than is needed. A good checklist is included in Figure 4.3. Recommended by Bikecentennial, it includes everything you will need for a cross-country trip. The only things to be added are those things you cannot live without. For example, if you are a photographer on special assignment, you will need many pounds of camera equipment. I came across one fellow from Japan riding on the Trans-America Trail with 70 pounds of stuff!

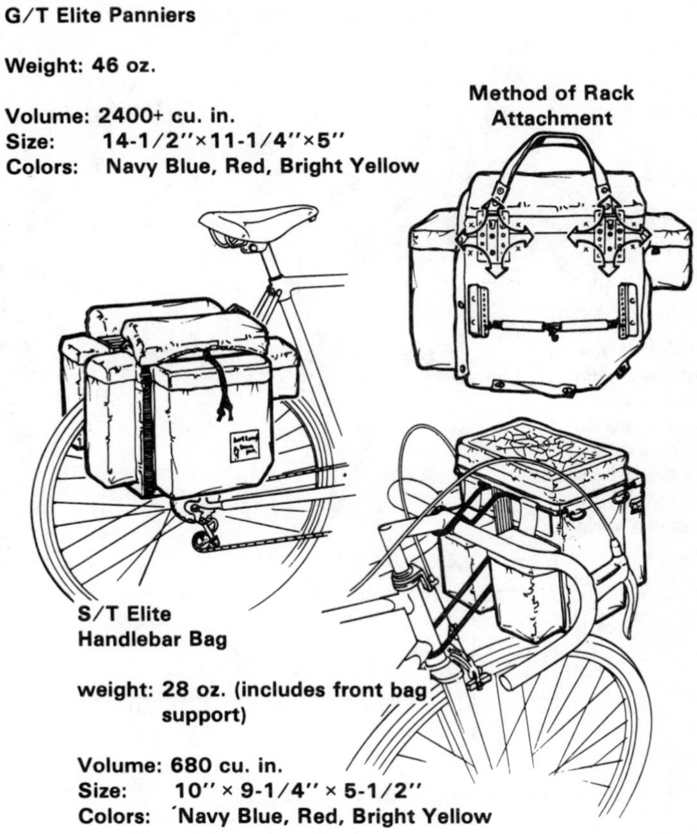

G/T Elite Panniers

Weight: 46 oz.

Volume: 2400+ cu. in.
Size: 14-1/2"×11-1/4"×5"
Colors: Navy Blue, Red, Bright Yellow

**Method of Rack
Attachment**

**S/T Elite
Handlebar Bag**

**weight: 28 oz. (includes front bag
        support)**

Volume: 680 cu. in.
Size: 10" × 9-1/4" × 5-1/2"
Colors: ´Navy Blue, Red, Bright Yellow

FIGURE 4.1   Kirtland Panniers

And that did not include the weight of his front, rear and middle panniers which were made out of heavy cowhide. He had a complete wardrobe, cooking pots, cameras, guitar, and tennis racket; he was ready for every contingency.

Whenever you can trim off an ounce, do so, because those ounces have a way of becoming pounds. If you should leave home with extras, you can always mail them back. You will be amazed at how little equipment you will actually need. Strive for a weight of 30 pounds or less.

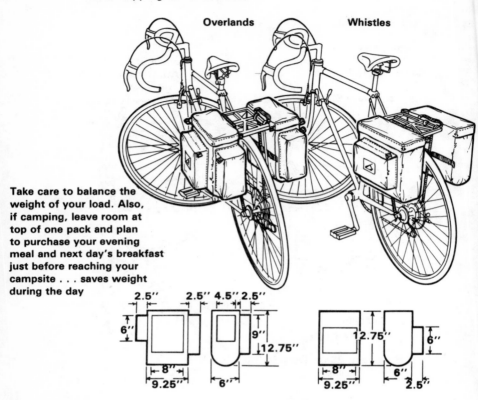

Take care to balance the weight of your load. Also, if camping, leave room at top of one pack and plan to purchase your evening meal and next day's breakfast just before reaching your campsite . . . saves weight during the day

FIGURE 4.2   Cannondale Rear Panniers

FIGURE 4.3   Equipment Checklist

Bicycle Equipment	Kitchen
Pump	Can opener
Rear carrier	Stove
Saddlebags	Eating utensils
Handlebar bag	Fuel bottle and fuel
Water bottles (1-3)	Pot(s)
Lock and heavy cable	Pot scrubber
Safety triangle or safety flag	Dishwashing soap
Tool kit*	Water purification tablets

The Bedroom
Tent (with good rain fly)
Sleeping bag
Foam pad
Ground cloth
Inner sheet sleeping sack

For Traveling Light
Pump
Water bottle
Screwdriver
Pliers
Six-inch adjustable (crescent) wrench
Tire irons
Tube repair kit
Small First-Aid kit
Sleeping bag and ground cloth (optional)
Change of clothes
Rain parka or poncho
Hat for sun protection
Ditty bag (toilet articles)

Miscellaneous
Cycling gloves
2 Hats — wool cap, summer sun shade, and always a helmet
Sunglasses, goggles
Glacier cream, suntan lotion, or sun screen
First-Aid Kit
Insect repellent
Sewing kit, small scissors
Candle or light
Nylon cord (at least 15 feet)
Toilet paper
Maps
Pocket knife
Camera and film

Clothes Closet
Cycling shorts (or equivalent)
1 pair long pants
2 short-sleeve shirts
1 long-sleeve shirt
2 or 3 pairs socks
2 or 3 sets underwear (optional)
Wool sweater
Windbreaker (breathable)
Rain parka or cape
Bathing suit and cap (optional)
Shoes (sturdy, sport shoe)
Sandals (or extra pair of shoes)
Towel (small, not white)
Toilet articles

*Tool Kit includes:
6" crescent
Freewheel remover
Chain link breaker, chain oil
2 tire irons
Patch kit
Spare inner tube
Screwdriver
Allen wrenches (if needed)
"Y" Box wrench/8,9, 10 mm

The checklist is rather self-explanatory because many of the items are either obviously specialty items or very limited in choice. I would like to comment on your tool kit contents. If your bicycle is in excellent shape before you leave, you should not need many tools. If it is just so-so, you could not carry enough tools. You should have a freewheel remover, two tire irons, tire patch kit, six inch crescent wrench, "Y"-shaped socket wrench with eight, nine, and ten millimeter ends, chain link remover, chain oil, needle-nosed pliers (optional), screw driver, and philips screw driver. I carry the screw driver items as part of my knife, a Swiss army pocket model. If you will be boxing your bike for transport you may need additional tools like allen wrenches. You should also find out what special tools your bike might require that are not included on this list. I met or heard about a number of tourists who also carried extra parts like another freewheel, extra chainrings, spare derailleurs, brake pads and cables, and extra bearings. To each his own! I did carry a larger extra chain ring with the idea of changing it for the ride across Kansas, but I did not use it.

Clothes Closet

The clothes closet is to me one of the more important categories and one to which you should give much thought. It is surprising how easily the weight can accumulate here if you are not careful because the choices are endless.

Summer and Winter Clothes

When riding the entire Trans-America Trail, you will need a summer and a winter set of clothes. If you begin in Oregon, you will have to carry both sets as far as Pueblo, where the winter items could be mailed home. Conversely, if you start in Virginia, save some weight by having some warmer clothes waiting for you in the Pueblo Post Office. Pueblo is mentioned as a dividing line between summer and winter on the Trail because west of Pueblo you are almost continuously at altitudes over

6,000 feet, and you should prepare for winter conditions. A June snowstorm is not uncommon in the Rockies, especially around Hoosier Pass, Togwotee Pass, Yellowstone, the Tetons, or the Cascades. Quite frequently night temperatures can drop down to 40 °F or less.

Summer clothes are easy to select, because by nature they are lightweight. Just be sure to include one lightweight cotton shirt with long sleeves. There will be sunny days when your arms will thank you. It is the winter clothes where the right decision is all-important. They cannot be heavy or bulky, but they must be warm. A good quality lightweight wool sweater is expensive, but it is worth the warmth when you are snowbound in the Tetons or the Cascades. Wool retains warmth even when wet, but synthetics do not. You should think in terms of many layers of lightweight clothes rather than one bulky sweater. You have better control over your comfort range when you can add or subtract a lightweight sweater. Down- or dacron-filled parkas or vests are also ideal. In fact, they are an excellent addition to your winter wardrobe.

Gloves are a necessity, especially during chilly mornings. It is really wise to have a pair of wool gloves and a pair of waterproof mittens to wear over them for those days when you get caught in a cold rain or snowstorm. (It *can* and *does* snow in the mountains in June.) You should also have a wool ski-type cap which will cover your ears.

Always select clothes that do not look like you slept in them. Wrinkle-free clothes, those you never have to iron, look so much neater. Clothes take quite a beating when they are shoved into panniers day after day. If you fold and then roll your things and stand them on end in the bag, they will survive much better. Everything is visible when you open the pannier, and you do not have to remove a lot of things to get to what you want. Some thought should also be given to color. Select bright colors like reds and yellows that can be seen easily when you ride. This is one of the safest precautions you can take. If you color coordinate your wardrobe so that everything is interchangeable, you will have a wider wardrobe with fewer items. Only by experimenting will you find combinations of winter and summer clothes that suit your personal preferences.

Goggles are something you may never need, but if you ride a 27-mile fast downhill into a snowstorm, you will be glad you have them, especially if they have clear or yellow lenses.

Rain Gear

Rain gear is always open to debate whenever a group of bikers gets together. I will preface my selection by saying that there are refreshing rains, and there are cold, nasty, and miserable rains. For the former, why bother with anything? Get wet and enjoy. It is the other kind that you try to prepare for. One argument goes something like this: If you wear a parka, it cannot breathe, and you are going to get wet underneath due to perspiration. So use a cape. But, according to the other opinion, capes are windbreakers, they flap all over the place, can get caught in the spokes and wheels, and you still get wet from underneath if your bike doesn't have fenders. Everyone has their own reasons. What you will have to do is discover what you prefer by experimenting. I personally do not like capes; however, I am not a hot-blooded person, and I can remain comfortable in a parka (Kelte makes a good one) especially during a cold, chilling rain. I prefer my own body heat and moisture to that of freezing rain any day, thank you. Gore-tex, a brand-new material, is waterproof and breathable. It is *very expensive*, but is absolutely the best solution to the problem so far.

To keep the legs dry, chaps work as well as anything, if you wear a parka or cape. It is not necessary to have full rain pants since the parka or cape covers that part of your anatomy anyway. Here, too, is where fenders are beautiful. No splashing from underneath, and you pedal along quite high and dry. Keeping the feet dry has been a problem. Until now the common trick was to tie a plastic bag over each foot. Sometimes they worked, but usually they did not. All you really hoped for was to stay warm anyway. Now Cool Gear has come out with a pair of very lightweight, waterproof booties with elastic tops and velcrol closures and openings on the soles for cleats.

Shoes

While we are on the subject of footwear, there are several different ways to go when selecting cycling shoes. Since you are on a
tour and will do a certain amount of walking to see the sights, a
sturdy tennis shoe is preferred over regular leather soled or
cleated cycle shoes, unless you want to carry an extra pair of
walking shoes and be forever changing. It is better to have a pair
of rubber thongs as extra shoes. They come in very handy
whenever you find yourself in a public shower. Thongs keep
your feet up off the germs of athlete's foot and whatever else
might be lurking in the dark shower stall corners.

Packing

Now that you have accumulated a mountain of paraphernalia,
the next step is to pack it so that you can find everything in the
dark and so that the weight is balanced in the bags and on the
bike.

Until you have developed a system, you will spend the first
couple of days hunting, rearranging, and exasperated. The main
thing is that you eventually learn to put an item back into the
same place each time as soon as you finish using it. Many small
valuable items, such as the pocket knife or insect repellent, get
left behind because they were put on the log instead of back in
their proper places.

Large items go in large pockets, and small items, in small
pockets. That is logical, isn't it? Heavy things should go on the
bottom to keep the center of gravity as low as possible. This will
make your bike easier to handle. An equal amount of weight
should be put on both sides, and the total weight divided into
one-third in the handlebar bag and two-thirds in the rear bags.
If all the load is added to the rear wheel, the front wheel will
tend to float and produce speed wobble. If you overload the
front wheel, it will become almost impossible to steer and balance safely and effectively.

All your valuables should be kept in the handlebar bag. Since
it is easily removed, you can take it with you whenever you leave

your bike. In my bag I carry my camera and camera accessories, money, chapstick, comb, first-aid kit, knife, hat or cap, and gloves.

You will also be using bungee straps to tie down things like a tent and sleeping bag. Bungee straps snap back like rubber bands. When stretching these "sling shots," you should hold onto it somewhere at midpoint with one hand as you are pulling on the hook end with the other. Make sure it is securely attached before letting go of it completely, and by all means do not get your head over the line of stretch. All this is to alert you to the possibility that you could get a nasty whack on your head — or worse, hit an eye — should it let go.

Once everything is secured on your bicycle, you will have an awkward, heavy bicycle, and not the sleek lightweight you started with. It takes a while to become accustomed to it, especially when stopping, starting, walking or pushing it, and riding over gravel roads. Riding on level pavements is not much different than when the bike was not loaded, except that you probably have it in a lower gear. You should also get into the habit of shifting into a still lower gear just prior to stopping at a red light, for example, so that it will be easier to start up again. You can then shift into the normal riding gear once you are underway.

Handling the loaded bicycle under various conditions such as on mountains and gravel roads will be discussed in the following chapter.

5

The Last-Minute Panic —
Getting into Condition

For many experienced bicyclists, undertaking a tour is nothing more than an extension of their regular riding activities. Knowing you are in top physical condition is very gratifying, and almost anyone can achieve that goal if certain exercise and conditioning programs are followed.

Never start out on a bicycle tour without first getting or being in shape for it. You should begin physical conditioning at least 30 days before your trip. If you do it correctly and regularly, you should be able to ride 50 miles a day easily and comfortably.

Selecting a Conditioning Program

The type of conditioning program selected will depend upon present physical routine, age, and general health conditions. After a few days of riding, the time or distance of your rides can gradually be increased. It is not necessary that you ride every day, but you should follow a regular routine. This is much more important than the number of miles covered. Whatever program is selected, the number of miles should be increased in easy steps: 20 miles is a much harder jump from 10 miles than it would be from 15 miles. You should keep pushing to gain endurance, and during at least part of your daily rides, think of doing five or ten minutes of extra exertion. Your stamina will not be increased if you always pedal at the same rate and expend the same amount of energy.

Although it is impossible to make any bicycle exercise program recommendations without knowing an individual's present physical condition, the following suggested programs are designed to achieve the physical condition required to make a long distance bicycle tour pleasurable and easy. They should only be used as a starting point, and adaptations should be made to fit your personal ability and stamina. At all times you should practice good form in ankling, spinning, cadence, and shifting. In this way you will condition all parts of your body together.

Program One in the third and fourth weeks would be for someone who has been a fairly active cyclist prior to deciding to go on tour (see Figure 5.1).

FIGURE 5.1   Program One

1st week	5 miles per day
2nd	Add 10 pounds to the bike and ride 5 miles per day in 30 minutes. Increase the mileage to 10 miles per day by week's end.
3rd	25 miles in 3 hours at least 3 times and increase the load to 30 pounds.
4th	50 miles in 8 hours at least 2 times with a 30 pound load or 50 miles in 5 hours with no load.

Program Two is more for the individual who has allowed his bicycle to collect dust and cobwebs for sometime (see Figure 5.2). It is up to you to decide how many total miles you care to ride each day with this program.

Regardless of which bicycling program is selected, it would first be a good idea to have your doctor perform an electrocardiogram under stress. With that information you will be better

FIGURE 5.2   Program Two

1st week	1 mile in 6-10 minutes for 4 or 5 days.
2d	2 miles in 10-15 minutes for 4 or 5 days.
3d	3 miles in 15-17 minutes for 4 or 5 days.
4th	4 miles in 20-22 minutes for 4 or 5 days.
5th	5 miles in 26-30 minutes for 4 or 5 days.

able to apply yourself to exercise. For exercise to do any good, you should increase your pulse rate about 75 percent over the maximum beats recorded during the EKG (electrocardiogram).

The heart rate chart given in Table 5.1 is yet another guide, and you can supplement this general conditioning advice with the chart given in Table 5.2 (times are given in minutes).

TABLE 5.1   Heart Rate Chart

Years of Age	Average Maximal Heart Rate (MHR)	Target Heart Rates During Each Training Period (30-45 minutes) Average (70% MHR)	Peaks (85% MHR)
15	210	147	179
20	200	140	170
25	195	137	166
35	185	130	157
45	175	123	149
55	170	119	145
65	165	116	140

TABLE 5.2   Riding Schedule

	1st Week	2nd Week	3rd Week	4th Week
Sunday	60	60	60	60
Monday	15	15	15	15
Tuesday	35	60	60	60
Wednesday	15	30	15	30
Thursday	60	60	60	60
Friday	15	15	15	15
Saturday	50	60	120	120

At least once, and preferably twice, during the final month, you should go on a 50 to 60 mile weekend tour with the same load you plan to carry on your big trip. You also will be able to learn how well your bike can or cannot handle the load. Of additional importance, this trip will give you a good opportunity to make sure that the gearing combination you selected is right for you.

Prepare for Varied Terrain and Conditions

During your training program, you should select a varied terrain for your route. Have you ever ridden your bicycle over a mountain? Through a snow storm? In the rain? Have you ever experienced fog or been out on very cold mornings? All these experiences can be a part of the Trail. In the case of mountains and rain, they are a part of it. The Trans-America Trail is not exactly a flat ride, but with the proper equipment and gears it is not difficult for a cyclist in adequate condition to handle. Selecting as varied a terrain as possible will give you the chance to perfect many of the necessary riding skills. And always remember to maintain 70 to 85 rpm cadence. Although you may still experience a certain amount of discomfort, your body will continue to improve its condition with each passing day for the first few days of your tour. If you have prepared well, your tour will be liberating, not debilitating.

Mountains

You will find that your fully loaded bicycle requires lower gears than when you attacked that same hill unloaded. Take your time. There are those riders who think they must "muscle" their way uphill in gears much too high for any enjoyment. Leave those gears to the racers or time trialers. You will have an easier time of it if you can relax and maintain a "jogger's" pace instead of grinding your way up. Select gears that allow you to use a reasonably fast cadence.

Descents are fun and reward all your efforts, but they require total concentration. Downhill is no place for long views of flowers and scenery. You should have been doing that on your slower uphill ride. Make certain your brakes are working! You should check to be sure your load is secure. Use caution. On steep downhills you can easily reach speeds of 40 to 50 mph and more. Brakes should be used lightly for control; they should be alternately pumped instead of having continuous pressure applied. The heat buildup could be enough to blow the tires, and that could be fatal. Patches of debris and rocks that could throw you should be watched for. Avoid sharp turns that can upset you because of your added load. Keep your body low by riding on the drops of your handlebars with at least two fingers on the brake levers to decrease your reaction time should you have to brake either for control or to stop suddenly. Slow down before a curve and lean into your turns. Around curves, get into the habit of bringing the inside pedal to the up position to eliminate the chance of hitting the pavement with the pedal. In many cases you will be matching or exceeding speed limits. You should consider your bicycle just like a motor vehicle at those times and use all of your lane if need be for safety. This does not mean weaving back and forth, however. I try to think in terms of a motorcycle and move out into the middle of the lane when I am traveling as fast or faster than the motor vehicles.

A rearview mirror is especially useful at these times because the wind is rushing past your ears so fast that you cannot hear the sounds of traffic behind you unless they blow a horn. The shock and surprise value of that could cause you to lose control. To know what is behind you, use a mirror.

With all this advice you are probably thinking that downhills are no fun. Like all bicycling skills, riding down mountain grades requires practice. Eventually, you will apply the necessary skills without thinking; and then the faster the downhill, the more you will enjoy it. But no downhill is fun if you should run out of control and hurt yourself.

Ozark-Type Hills and Rolling Terrain

These areas are much like mountains except that your climbs and descents are, of course, much shorter. In these situations, you will be required to shift much more frequently to maintain pedal cadence. The one rule of thumb to remember is to down shift before you have to. In that way an upgrade will not catch you in a too high gear, your cadence will not be broken, nor will you be putting unnecessary strain on the shifting mechanisms by trying to shift while struggling against increased pedal resistance.

Gravel Roads

Gravel roads require a special technique even if you are not riding a fully loaded bicycle. If they are hard-packed with no stones or large rocks, it is a joy to behold them, but those kinds just do not exist! The dirt roads on the Trans-America Trail — of which there are at least 100 total miles and never less than 20 miles at any one stretch — are from fair to poor. But you can cope with them and even enjoy yourself if you know how to alter your riding style accordingly.

First, I like my toe straps loose in case the bike begins to wallow in the loose stuff. That way I can catch my balance in a hurry by putting a foot down if need be. Second, gear down into a very low gear so that you can really spin the pedals especially through sand. The added gyroscopic effect aids your balance. Since your forward speed is much less on gravel, this effect will give your wheels some additional assistance in balancing. Third, ride low by using the drops of the handlebars for better steering control and a lower center of gravity. Fourth, when going downhill on gravel, slide as far back on the seat as possible thereby putting as much weight as possible on the rear wheel. Fifth, never use your front brakes alone, as that will cause the bike to slide out from under you. Get in the habit of using just the rear brake; touch the front one only when you have complete control of the bike and its braking travel. Do not allow your speed to build up so that you are racing out of control. Last, remember that the dirt on these roads can be deeper on the outside or high point of the curves.

Rain

If there is a summer shower, you may choose to wait it out. But if the day has been a hot one, it is sort of nice to enjoy the soaking for its cooling and invigorating qualities. Whatever you do, remember that the streets are their slickest at the rain's beginning. It takes time for the other vehicles to "wash" away the accumulated road oils. Spray from passing cars can leave you momentarily blinded, and a heavy downpour is hard on your eyes. For those times you should have some kind of eye protection like clear or yellow goggles, and if you wear bright colors like yellow, you will be visible in the gloom.

Night Riding

The rule for this is simple: avoid it. If you do find yourself out after dark, you should have a good headlight and plenty of reflectors — front and rear.

Cattle Guards

Easterners have never heard of them, but cattle guards are the westerner's answer to the sewer grate. They are evenly spaced metal pipes across the width of the road running perpendicular to the road. They keep the cows from visiting the neighbors. You can ride over most of them if the spacing is not too wide. You should not make any sudden turns for obvious reasons and should maintain a steady pace. If in doubt, get off and walk your bike across.

The Buddy System

There are a number of reasons why it is fun to ride with a "buddy" rather than solo. An obvious one, of course, is to have somebody to talk to. On very long trips — more than one week

— it gets rather lonesome after a while, and you can look out for each other. On long, tedious days or late afternoon hill climbs, it is nice to have someone to commiserate with.

Food buying becomes easier because many things are packaged for at least two people. Splitting and sharing the load is another reason: half as many tools, one stove, half the tent weight, for starters. Just make sure that you both ride at about the same speed and endurance.

This is not to say that you must always ride within talking or even shouting distance. Bicycling is basically a solo endeavor, and its joys come from an aloneness and oneness with the passing scene. Having someone constantly beating on your eardrums detracts from these pleasures. Rather, a buddy should be a good companion who is reliable, responsible, and compatible, but who is not always needing to be in sight. As long as a buddy shows up at the prearranged meeting points, consider that the extent of your buddy's riding duties. And you should do the same for your buddy.

6

Bed and Board

Once you are on your way, where to eat and sleep become very important concerns, and both directly involve the question of money. If you are going self-contained, with tent and sleeping bag, the bed part is easy. A good spot sheltered by trees, bushes, or old buildings or an official campground should be found preferably no later than five or six P. M., and should be set up. Food is a different situation especially if you are on a limited budget. If you manage well, you can travel on $3.50 a day (1977 inflation). It has been done, and that includes everything except excesses. You will have to plan well, do your own cooking, and regard restaurants as a once in a great while luxury with the exception of breakfast. That should be your most substantial meal to keep you going all day. For the price of a meal, breakfasts in restaurants are the best buy. Some bikers prefer that idea because it means getting an earlier start away from camp by not having to mess with the chores of cooking.

Food Tips

Your eating habits will and should change when you are riding a bicycle 50 or more miles for days on end. Your desire for carbohydrates increases so you should include peanut butter, spaghetti, bananas, and pears, for example, in your travel diet. Leafy, green salads will begin to rate high on your list of favorite things especially after a hard or long ride when you have depleted your potassium reserves. The only time I ate in a restaurant was because I wanted a chef's salad.

Certain things happen to your body during strenuous physical activity and knowing this will better enable you to select and maintain a healthful, proper diet while on the road.

The six most important nutrients to keep under control are carbohydrates, fats, proteins, minerals, vitamins, and water. Your muscles work because of carbohydrate reserves which convert into glycogen. Carbohydrates are most important to you as a cyclist. If they are depleted, you will become fatigued. Fats take over when carbohydrates are used up, but they are slower in breaking down. Proteins are body builders which help your tissues and bones repair themselves. Minerals help muscular action and oxygen consumption. There are six minerals which cyclists should be aware of: calcium for heart muscle and rhythmic beat; phosphorus to help the body release energy; and sodium and potassium to maintain fluid balance and to transmit muscle impulses. Magnesium transmits nerve impulses and triggers muscle contractions. Iron helps carry oxygen, and without it, you feel weak.

To put this into practical terms, you will desire and should eat fresh fruits and vegetables often. They are very high in carbohydrates. Potatoes will satisfy your craving for starches. Peanut butter and honey replace fats, proteins, and sugar reserves. Milk should be drunk for vitamin D and calcium. Certain dried fruits are also high in carbohydrates. Dried apricots and raisins, for example, have iron in large amounts. Meats contain no carbohydrates, but they do have protein and fat. So do nuts, whole grains, and cereals, but they also contain carbohydrates and are therefore the better choice.

The more a food product is removed from its natural state the less nutritional value it contains. For example, canned carrots offer less value than freshly cooked carrots and much less than raw carrots. Junk food should be avoided in all forms. You are only wasting money for empty calories. Since much junk food is deep fried, you are adding the problem of making your digestive system work overtime. You will be very uncomfortable if you face a hard mountain climbing ride with your stomach full of hamburger and fries topped off with a Coke. In addition, junk food is high in simple sugars. To overload your system in this way will induce a reactionary hypoglycemia that is characterized by, of all things, hunger pangs. The less you eat the better you will ride, and that is always true. When your stomach is working overtime to digest all that food, there is no energy left over for your muscles to pedal the bicycle.

Most Americans overeat as it is, and cycling is no excuse for overindulgence. In fact, many top athletes such as runners and cycle racers not only limit their caloric intake, but fast at least three or four days every month while maintaining their regular training. The reason for the fast is to teach the body to become proficient in using its stored energy — fat. It also helps maintain the lightness of body weight which makes for more efficient performance with less effort. In simple terms, you will find it easier to pedal uphill if you do not have any excess body fat to haul along. It is not unusual for bikers to expound on their super light, lightweight bicycles for which they paid dearly, defeating it all by being 20 pounds overweight.

When to buy your food will obviously depend on where you are in relation to the next food store and where you plan to camp. There are times when you will decide to explore the back roads and not show your face to civilization again for days. Those times will require special planning, and you will need such things as nuts, hard sausage like beef jerky, cheese, tinned meat or fish, and dried fruit. Usually a store is within a day's ride. To save weight, make your purchases just before camping for the night. Of course, you will have to know where that last store is in relation to camp. It is never a bad idea to have at least one day's supply of emergency food rations just in case.

This is one of the times when group travel has a certain advantage. Ever try to purchase just enough fresh salad makings for one person? It cannot be done. It is the same when planning lunch. How long does it take you to eat a loaf of bread? For additional cooking and meal planning ideas two publications worth reading are "The Bicycle Tourist's Cookbook" published by Bikecentennial and *Roughing It Easy* by Dian Thomas.

There are stretches along the western half of the Trans-America Trail which are high and dry — deserts in other words. For people not accustomed to this climate, no amount of water is enough. But where there is a will, there is a way. You can always flag down motor homes, pickup trucks, or beg or borrow from your friend, but you will make it. Usually, two pint bottles should see you through. If in doubt after checking your map and realizing that the Sierra desert exists between you and the next town, get another plastic container and fill it before you leave town.

Unless you *know* you are above all forms of civilization including livestock, do not drink from those deceivingly crystal clear, cold streams. Hepatitis is not much fun. There were very few times when we did enjoy the pleasures of a bygone time. Today you should carry those evil, foul tasting water purification tablets or a mechanical water purifier. The latest, slickest thing for purifying water is called an Argenion (Model MKT II). It is a very small, lightweight (less than four ounces) version of a deluxe motor home setup. It can filter up to 1,500 gallons of water with no nasty before- or after-tastes.*

Certain fruits such as pears, oranges, and raisins, are also high in water content. They can carry you a long way, and you should always have one or two items tucked away.

In the last year or so a new drink product has hit the market. Called ERG, which means "electrolyte replacement with glucose," it is an isotonic sugar solution. It makes for a quick and painless absorption of electrolytes and fluid because its chemical

*They can be ordered from Marketers International, 3711 N. 75th St., Scottsdale, Arizona 85251.

makeup matches your body's own plasma and perspiration. If this still sounds complicated and involved, ERG is nothing more than a form of perspiration. Other so-called thirst quenchers like Gatorade are hypertonic. The results quite frequently are stomach and muscle cramps and a temporary systemic dehydration.

ERG was developed over several years by Bill Gookin — chemist, life-sciences teacher, and marathon runner. It now comes in three different flavors: lemonade, fruit punch, and competition which has no after-taste. The competition flavor seems to be the most popular.

To Camp or Not To Camp

I prefer camping because it seems most compatible with the idea of bicycle travel. Self-sufficiency and self-containment are not appealing to all individuals, however. The next step up is the bike inn which Bikecentennial secured at cities and towns within comfortable riding distances along the length of the trail. They vary from plush to primitive, but they are a form of shelter which eliminates the need for a tent. You still need a foam pad and a sleeping bag. Most do have simple army cots. The buildings are school gyms, college dorms, churches, VFW halls, and the like, and you are responsible for your food preparation. In most cases, cooking is not allowed inside the buildings.

First class, of course, is the motel/hotel route with nothing more on your bike than a toothbrush and change of clothes. Just be sure you have lots of money. The only advantage I can justify is the nightly shower. However, it is the rare campground which does not also have shower facilities.

Most bikers camp. Aside from the expense, there is something very soul-satisfying to know that you can travel wherever the road may carry you with no need for civilization, except to buy your daily food supplies. Then, too, compared to watching the glow of the motel TV, watching the sun set behind a snow covered peak while listening to the evening birdsongs is more visually rewarding and mentally peaceful.

You should have a waterproof and lightweight tent for those days when it is rainy and cold or if you are in mosquito country. Camplife can be quite uncomfortable without one. They are expensive, costing over $100 for a small tent, but five to ten motel nights will equal that expense. You will want a lightweight piece of plastic or a space blanket for a ground cloth. It keeps ground moisture away from you and protects the bottom of your tent. A sleeping bag as light as two pounds ten ounces will keep you warm at 25 °F. Camp 7 makes such a bag in a mummy style. If you add a foam pad or air mattress of some sort, your bedroom is complete. For the privilege of watching sunrises and shooting stars, you will carry from eight to ten extra pounds.

Where to camp is probably the major concern of each day. If there are established campgrounds in the area, you can always check in there. But what if there are none? The problem is not as difficult as it may seem to the fledgling camper especially if one is west of the Mississippi River. Here the land is much more open, towns are further apart, population is considerably less, fences are more for keeping livestock in rather than people out, and much of the land is either state or national forest. Little room is needed for camping — an out of the way place either down a path, lane, or side road with trees, tall bushes, or other groundcover is perfect. It is often wise not to tell the world where you are spending the night whether you are alone or not. In fact, the only time I consider a commercial campground is when there is a group of four or more bikers.

Another good possibility is around deserted buildings. In Oregon, I spent a delightful late evening and night on the side porch of a recently abandoned Victorian farmhouse. If these possibilities do not present themselves, then you can consider a friendly farmer's side yard. Going up to him and asking if he knows of any good camping areas will usually result in an invitation: "Why, you all can stay right here if ya a mind to."

Churches with rectories are another good bet. So are graveyards. If you do not mind the "ghosts," they make for very quiet neighbors. Short of that, small town city parks quite often have an area where you can spend the night, but you should ask first and be sure the local constable knows you are there. If you are a member of the League of American Wheelmen, be sure to take your membership directory with you. It is an unlimited source of potential places to spend the night, plus you will have something in common. And I ask you, would a biker ever turn away another biker?

The last idea I can come up with if all else fails is to consider spending the night in the city jail. All towns, large or small, have a jail, and in small towns the most activity they usually see is the local town drunk. There is a good chance that the night you pedal into their life you will have the jail all to yourself. This would be a most unusual experience, to say the least. In fact, the police department can be very helpful in finding you a place to stay. If not in jail, then a possibility is their front lawn or at the chief's house.

I stated earlier that you should plan to arrive or make camp no later than 6:00 P. M. This allows ample time to find a spot to pitch your tent or lay your sleeping bag. Finding a soft, level spot after dark can be quite tedious. Finding firewood, even when abundant, and cooking after dark are also difficult. By ending your riding at an early hour you will be able to complete all camp, cooking, and clean-up chores while there is still daylight, and you can enjoy the sunset and spend the night relaxed. Camping activity that is not leisurely is no fun.

Unless there is a lot of dead wood in the area, you should forget about any fires other than the one generated by your small gas stove. Although a fire is nice for cooking (the coals are much hotter than the flame) and creates evening atmosphere, it tends to isolate you from your surroundings. It is impossible to see beyond its glow. But if you must have a fire, keep it small like the Indians did rather than the present-day white man's gigantic bonfire.

Only fallen dead wood, which can be very scarce in established campgrounds, should be collected. Often you can purchase it or get a free supply from the campground manager. Branches should never be cut off a living tree or bush and the fire should be made in designated areas only. How many times have you come upon not one fire pit but several, all within a few feet of each other? This is a very destructive practice and totally unnecessary when the orginal fire pit would have served all who followed.

To Your Health, Comfort, and Cleanliness

Even if you camp every day, you should keep yourself and your clothes as clean as possible, and that is not as difficult as it may seem. There is no excuse for a dirty person. Most commercial campgrounds have shower and laundry facilities, as do many state and national campgrounds. You can also check into using the showers at the city's public swimming pool or asking a motel manager if for 50 cents or so you could use one of his showers. Usually they say yes. Carry such things as witch hazel (it does wonders for your feet) and dry skin cream and lip balm for general comfort. Keep a small towel handy for a midday rinse. The cleaner you are, the healthier you will remain.

Take a day out to rest every week or so. It is also good to take a short break at least once every hour. One should not ride for long stretches during the heat of the day. Time should be taken to enjoy the scenery you heard so much about — that is one of the reasons you are touring, isn't it?

Accept windy days in a relaxed manner and with the attitude that the wind will change direction sooner or later. Most cyclists will tell you they would rather ride uphill than into the wind. This is a state of mind. You know that there is a top to that hill with a down side so you ride relaxed. Not so with the wind because you know that it will probably blow all day. When you are on flat land and want to go as fast as you normally do, you push harder to get through the day and end up wearing yourself out both mentally and physically.

Adjust the layers of your clothing to fit your daily personal comfort. Climbing hills is a sweaty experience. Stop and remove all unnecessary clothes until you reach the top. Reverse the procedure for the descent so that you will not become chilled. This is where a pullover windbreaker is a handy item to carry along.

Drink liquids before you are thirsty, and eat before you are hungry. Frequent snacking is much better than three large daily meals. Your chances of becoming ill are less if you are in good physical condition before leaving home. Some of the more common problems that do arise are constipation and diarrhea, both of which could be caused by changes in routine and schedule. Other causes are improper diet and impure water. Eating fresh fruits and vegetables and avoiding soda pop will usually correct these problems.

Forewarned Is Forearmed

You should know how to recognize signs of other illnesses which, although not common, can and do occur to the unwary. Most common are heat exhaustion, heat stroke, and hypothermia. All three are related in that your body is reacting adversely and defensively to weather conditions.

Heat exhaustion occurs when your water intake is inadequate and cannot compensate for fluids lost through sweating. You will feel weak, tired, dizzy, and possibly nauseous; continue to sweat profusely; and your skin will feel clammy. You may faint, have a headache, and perhaps cramps. If you suspect you are in that state, drink sips of salt water to replace what you lost, lie down in as cool a place as possible (like an air-conditioned room), or apply cool, wet cloths. If you vomit, you need help and should go to a hospital. For several days, you should take it easy and avoid abnormally warm temperatures.

Heat stroke is very serious — a matter of life or death. The body temperature can reach 106 °F or higher, and immediate cooling of the body is necessary. The skin will feel hot, red, and dry. There is no sweating, and pulse is rapid. Unconsciousness may occur.

Hypothermia occurs when body temperature is affected by cold. Your internal temperature drops, and you experience uncontrollable shivering. Death, believe it or not, will occur at no more than a lowering of only 6 °F from the normal 98.6 °F! Hypothermia is probably the most serious situation which could occur while you are out biking. It is imperative that you or one of your companions recognize and understand what is happening. What makes it so insidiously subtle is that hypothermia can occur in the mild temperatures of 30 to 50 °F. Many conditions can start the process. If the body has become wet through perspiration, rain, or a wet snowstorm, and the body loses heat faster than it produces it, hypothermia threatens — or occurs.

At only 2.5 °F below normal body temperature, shivering can begin. It is the body's way of trying to produce more heat. As the temperature continues to drop, coordination deteriorates to where you cannot even light a match to build a fire; you stumble; your speech is thick; finally you lose your memory and cannot even remember your own name.

Even the mildest symptoms demand immediate treatment. The ideal procedure is to submerge the victim in a tub of water heated to no more than 110 °F. If conscious, the victim should be made to drink large quantities of warm, heavily sugared liquids. Wet clothes should be removed, and the victim made as warm as possible. Shelter should be found out of the wind, and the victim put into a sleeping bag if possible.

Bikers should always keep their heads covered when they are out in the cold since one-half of the body's heat is lost through the head. Avoid exhaustion; and be sure you have enough to eat.

A sudden summer snowstorm in the mountains is more common than often thought. Twice on the Trans-America Trail my group rode in the snow. The first time was while crossing Togowotee Pass at only 9,000 feet in mid-June. I experienced the beginning signs of hypothermia and luckily I knew what to do. The other snowstorm was in July over Hoosier Pass.

part 2

The 4,300-Mile Summer

7

Background of the
Trans-America Trail

According to the Bikecentennial brochure:

> Leisure time is precious to each of us. Bicycle travel is ideal for those seeking adventure. It affords us the chance to reflect, to rekindle our spirit, and to travel with people of similar and dissimilar lifestyles. Our bodies need healthful exertion, and our minds need a chance to relax and grow.

There are roads in this country which reflect a bygone style of living which is all but forgotten. There are small, quiet towns, and the people who live in these small towns will take the time to share a smile and a greeting. The Trans-America Trail seeks out these places.

It took three years of research by a handful of dedicated bikers to find those hidden places. They established a trail of diversity and geographic variety to make the traveler aware of the land, its relationships and its contrasts to all living things.

Confined or defined by two oceans, the Trans-America Trail covers all segments of America from the rocky coast to the desert, the grasslands, the Rocky mountains, the Ozarks, the Appalachians, and finally the Bluegrass region of Kentucky and Virginia.

According to the Bikecentennial application:

> In its slow, meandering course across America, the Trans-America Trail traverses national forests, national parks, and takes in a cross-section of American life. It also captures much of America's early history, by paralleling or crossing the Lewis and Clark Trail, the Oregon Trail, and several other historic trails.
>
> The Bikecentennial organization has researched and developed the Trans-America Trail as a healthful, nonpolluting approach to meaningful adventure during the Bicentennial and in future years. The trail affords a close look at a varied terrain, an ever-changing climate, an independent people, and a fascinating panorama of rural America. But this is not the trail for everyone. It is a slow trail where emphasis is placed on group or individual experience, not on speed.

The concept was based on an ever-growing need for quiet places to bicycle. Because of the vast interstate highway system, many thousands of miles of roads are now bypassed, forgotten, and used only by local citizens to travel between small towns. These roads make up the backbone of the Trans-America Trail. These secondary country roads were chosen to give the cyclist an intimate relationship with the land and the people that the wide, noisy highways never give. Specially constructed bikeways were not part of the plans for several reasons. For one, they would be too isolating. The idea behind the Trans-America Trail was to find a good cross-country route on existing backroads which were already maintained and would initiate no further development costs. In the country, all towns and most houses face or have access to the roadway, which means that as a cyclist you will be passing by America's front door. Recent surveys have shown isolated bikepaths to be more hazardous than riding with traffic. These bikepaths are not kept clean and free of debris;

they are often poorly designed and always give a false sense of security. When that happens, people take chances because they are no longer as alert as they should be.

An Idea and its Repercussions

Certainly the four individuals — Dan and Lys Burden and June and Greg Siple — who were directly responsible for Bikecentennial had no inkling that their original idea would grow into such large proportions. With help from such sources as the U.S. Forest Service, the U.S. Department of Agriculture, the U.S. Department of Transportation, and the Bureau of Outdoor Recreation, to mention a few, the idea grew into reality. Financial support came from the American Revolution Bicentenial Association, the Montana Bicentennial Administration, and constituent members of the bicycle industry. The greatest support — both in human resources and in financial backing — has come from Bikecentennial members and volunteers across the U.S. and around the world.

There is a rather interesting story related by Lys Burden about how the original idea of Bikecentennial was conceived. In 1973 they were riding their bicycles from Alaska to Tierra del Fuego. Somewhere in a Mexican town called Chocolate, they were cooling their wheels and heads when the conversation went into a discussion of 1976, three years away. They would be home by then, and they wanted to do something in their own way to celebrate the Bicentennial. The idea of riding their bikes coast to coast sounded like fun. The idea grew: "We could invite a few friends along." It was decided to contact bike clubs throughout the country and invite *everybody*. It was settled, and all four were aglow with enthusiasm for their next big ride after Tierra del Fuego was conquered. The following morning one of the riders looked down at her odometer and it read by coincidence 1776! Bikecentennial had begun.

In 1976 over 4,000 bikers responded to Bikecentennial's invitation, and about 2,000 of them rode the entire 4,300 miles. In all, that amounted to over 11 million miles in just one summer. It was a unique Bicentennial celebration, but it did not end there. Additional routes are in various planning stages as offshoots from what has become the main trail (see Figure 7.1). There are or will be trails following the East coast and Pacific coast, the Mississippi River, and loop tours in Oregon, Idaho, Virginia, and Kentucky. In time it is anticipated that the Trans-America Trail will become the backbone of approximately 20,000 miles of carefully researched routes winding throughout all parts of the United States as well as portions of Canada and Mexico.

The selection and availability of food and lodging is also of major importance in planning a successful route. Detailed Bike-centennial maps and guidebooks have been assembled to aid the cyclist in this regard.

The Trail Itself

The Trail is divided into five main sections; there is a map and guidebook for each one. The guidebooks list information such as riding conditions which explain terrain and traffic conditions, average weather conditions during summer months, historical background, area geology, campgrounds and other types of ac-commodations, bike shops, and major points of interest in each area. There is also a chapter dealing with the plants which make up the natural environment of every section. The five sections are Coast Cascades, Rocky Mountains, Plains-Ozarks, Bluegrass, and the Appalachians. Each of these sections will be covered in detail in the following chapters. The material presented here is in addition to the guidebooks and is mainly presented to you as added incentive to experience the "ride of a lifetime" for your-self.

FIGURE 7.1   The Trans-America Bicycle Trail

THE TRANSAMERICA BICYCLE TRAIL

THE NEW KENTUCKY LOOP BICYCLE TRAIL

THE NEW OREGON LOOP BICYCLE TRAIL

THE NEW VIRGINIA LOOP BICYCLE TRAIL

THE NEW MONTANA/IDAHO LOOP BICYCLE TRAIL

For as many people who claim that west-to-east is best, you will find an equal number of proponents for the east-to-west ride. The argument stems mainly over wind directions. Theoretically, the prevailing winds in this country during the summer are out of the west. I tend to believe that, and my experience last summer bears me out. Seldom did I have a head wind, and I rode eastward. I have heard a few others complain though that they had nothing but headwinds. I contend that they found a freak situation, and it followed them or they followed it across the country. They should have waited until I caught up with them with my pushing winds and continual good luck all summer.

The Rocky Mountains are also easier riding going eastward. The western slopes are slightly steeper but much shorter than their eastern faces. And if you have a tail wind, these prevailing winds will help push you uphill. And what a lovely, long downhill you get each time. After crossing all the peaks and passes, you reach the Colorado Piedmont with many miles of downhill into the Plains. The same is true for the Virginia Piedmont. Again, there were miles of gradual downhill — this time to the sea. Although both ends of the trail begin at sea level, you will spend less time and miles of climbing if you begin in the west. There is one final reason for riding eastward: the sun is behind you, and it is much more pleasant this way than if you ride west into the sun all day. (Yet some riders tell me they prefer to have the rising sun warming their backs in the morning.)

The total mileage of the Trans-America Trail averages 4,300 — actually 4,281 or 4,457 depending upon whom you talk to. If you figure an average of 4,300 miles, then you can decide how many miles you can comfortably ride in a day — day after day. How long should it take? If you are not in a big rush, 90 days is a reasonable time and that is the time set by Bikecentennial. If you can do 100 miles day after day, then 50 to 54 days is about all the vacation time you will need. There are a number of non-riding or rest days included in that total. For the 90-day ride, it is recommended that you take 10–14 rest days, and 6–8 rest days are needed for the faster trip.

If you are fortunate enough to do the entire Trail at one time, you will collect a continuous stream of impressions and contrasts unbroken by time. They will form one vivid, exciting concept of the America you found. If time demands that you do only a section at a time, your final impressions will certainly be different than if you had completed the Trail all in one summer. But by all means go and experience and learn what you can. Someone said: "You only regret what you don't do."

Thomas Wolfe summed up the concept quite well by stating in essence: I am a part of all that I have touched and that has touched me. And that part, has no existence save that which I gave to it. As I change, so too does it.

The following five chapters explain and describe the Trail in detail. Each chapter corresponds to Bikecentennial's sections and dividing points. I believe that by doing it this way, it will be easier for you to coordinate the information found in their guidebooks and these chapters.

By contacting Bikecentennial, you can obtain copies of all the maps and guidebooks. In addition to their maps, I found it convenient to enter the route onto each state highway map as I went along. I like the idea of a total state overview and reference. If you decide to do likewise, try to get the most detailed state map possible. Your best bets are the official state maps produced by the state highway departments. Even then you will find some roads not on those maps, especially in Kentucky and Virginia because there are so many backroads from which to choose.

So, if you are ready, let's try to satisfy that wanderlust and go chase the gypsy spirit across America!

8

The Coast Cascades

To ride a bicycle is rhythm. It is complete, and needs nothing else.

From the rugged coastline of Oregon to the calmer Atlantic seaboard of Virginia, a 4,300-mile bicycle trail winds across the width, breadth, and heart of America. Bicycle touring has had a belated beginning in America, but at least it is a beginning. Bicycling is out there, beckoning you to discover all it has to offer.

The Flavor of Oregon

The forest primeval runs right to the salty sea, and the salty sea mingles with the smells of the pungent pine forest. Windblown low growing conifer-type shrubs hug the sand dunes all along the coast. Wind- and water-eroded rocks stand like sentinels amid the waves. Oregon is fog and mist and rain. Haze frequently covers the hilltops and hides in the lower valleys. Tall pines, clothed with lush moss and surrounded by huge specimens of skunk cabbage, cover millions of acres. Millions of acres have also been cleared leaving bald, eroded brown spots on the mountain sides — first all the trees are cut down and hauled away, and then when the rains come, the mountain is washed away.

Oregon is the land of the logging truck. The smell of pine lingers heavy in the air whenever one of them passes, 60-foot long logs swinging along behind. A tree neither dies with the first saw cut nor is it dead by the last; it takes a long time for a tree to die.

Unlike the Atlantic coast, Oregon's coast is extremely narrow, usually only two miles wide with the coastal range tight against the ocean's edge. Averaging about 4,000 feet in height, the mountains are a natural barrier for much of the rainfall. Fishing villages and summer resorts line the coast while peaceful farms are found just inland, giving a completely different feel to the

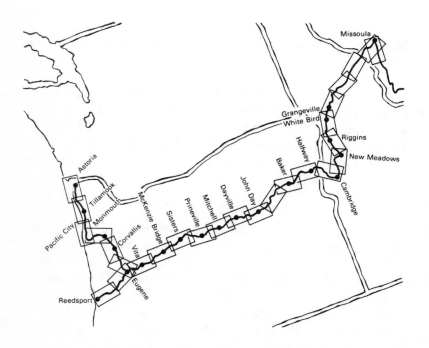

coastal life. The remains of clams and oysters are piled alongside the fish factories lining the estuaries, while the neighboring building could be a cheese factory. Tillamook, for example, is famous for its cheese. From nearby dairy farms scattered around the valley come raw materials.

The ride along the coast is rolling, with only a few challenging ascents, but the downhills reward your efforts. The steepest grade is over the top of Cape Lookout, but it is downhill almost all the way into Pacific City. With wide and free abandonment, the group of cyclists I was leading raced and swung along the coast with pine forests on our left and the salty air and wind-swept ocean surf on the right. We were a part of all that surrounded us, and we gave the scene a reality just as it gave something in return to us.

Food and lodging are readily available because of all the resorts which dot the coast. Campgrounds are also easily found. Oregon is not only a state free of litter, but it has some of the best campgrounds in the country. They are clean, grassy, and well-maintained parks. One, Cape Lookout State Park, is separated from the sea by a sand dune. It is a place to walk along the beach and savor the wind and mist. Lava and quartz met sand and formed an 800-foot sheer cliff which juts out into the sea. Rock fingers hold coves between them, waterfalls cascade among twisted trees, and moss-covered rocks and trees grow everywhere almost to the ocean. Sea gulls wheel about overhead, while the beach is littered with sand dollars, tiny shells, and birds' footprints.

My journal records:

> A fog bank is a few miles out over the ocean, and as the sun sets, colors too numerous to mention begin to play upon the water and sky above. While just offshore the bell buoys chime in unison. Spectacular views are everywhere, and from the higher points along the coast the view is limitless over the expanse of rock and water.

The morning of the fifth day we crossed Oxbow Divide, the first of six major passes in Oregon. Although this ride over the coastal range toward Salem is relatively easy, it made some people painfully aware of the fact that the Trans-America Trail is not flat.

The highest of the coastal range summits is a mere 820 feet. A number of delightful downhills are climaxed by a long descent into the Willamette Valley. The thing that causes a certain degree of unpleasantness along this stretch is the heavy traffic.

As soon as one heads inland, the coast is immediately left behind. In Oregon it is not a lingering thing. Dairy farms, orchards, and vegetable patches quickly take over. A beautiful valley on the far side of the coastal range is dotted with neat farm houses with rhododendron and lilacs in bloom. From Otis to Salem, the road is called the Van Duzer Corridor. It was once an Indian footpath, then a pioneer route, and later an army supply route for Fort Yamhill; today, it is a peaceful tree-lined road.

As you continue to move inland, the climate will become somewhat drier, and the mornings will be cooler at the higher elevations. Morning dewdrops make the pine needles sparkle while the skunk cabbage is skunking on the damp floor, smells intermingling with smells.

An interesting phenomenon, that takes a few days to appear, is the body's ability to adjust to a different measure of time. Most people are oriented to automobile speeds, so the first bicycling days seem extremely slow. To finally function within the beat and cadence of pedal strokes requires a slowing of mind to a different span of time and distance. When that finally happens, you are at one with what you are experiencing.

Easy riding continues along the floor of the Willamette Valley which is 40 to 60 miles wide. You follow little used country backroads, since most of the traffic is now over on the interstate. Every so often you come upon a small lumber mill or pulp processing plant, and by the smell of soggy paper, you can tell when one is nearby. The ring of saw blades fills the air, heralding Oregon's largest industry.

There is something very settled looking about this valley. Most farm buildings and towns look like they have been there a very long time. New construction is seldom seen, and weathered barns stand proudly upon the landscape. The crush of people and city congestion is also notably absent. The towns, all of which have a Main Street, are unhurried and friendly, everyone knowing or recognizing everyone else. Here people still have a face and an identity.

I recorded the following in my journal:

> Just outside Harrisburg, looking for a place to camp for the night, I found an abandoned farm. Every one of the buildings was still in excellent condition, as if it had only been a few months since the people moved away. The house had a front porch which wrapped around the side — complete with pillars — and I spread the sleeping bag out there for the night. The lilac bushes reached above the porch railing, the grass had gone wild, and the front gate hung open by a single unbroken hinge. There were several fruit trees in the sideyard with blossoms, and a family of starlings had a nest in a hole under the eaves. With a little effort, the place could have been as good as new. What a shame.

Eugene, according to Marshall Strickler, is "a *great* town. Everybody bikes or jogs or does both. Bike paths abound. Oregon allocates one percent of all highway revenues to developing and maintaining bike paths throughout the state, and in Eugene it shows."

There is an alternate route which begins in Reedsport and heads directly inland for Eugene. This will cut about three days off of your riding time, including the exciting 120 miles of coastline. From Reedsport to Gardiner and along the mouth of the Smith River, the cyclist will find very easy terrain. There are a few hills along the route, which winds through the dairy farms along the river flats. At this point, the Smith River is broad and placid. It is interesting to note that the Trans-America Trail parallels rivers for almost all of its route through the Rockies as far as Pueblo, Colorado. With the exception of Kansas and a few short stretches in the remaining states, rivers are a constant companion.

According the the Bikecentennial guidebook:

> Once inland, the terrain changes considerably. It is quite hilly from the beginning of the Siuslaw National Forest nearly all the way to Eugene. There are almost no services available between Gardiner and Eugene, a distance of almost 85 miles.

The Cascades begin to appear on the horizon after Springfield. There is a lovely, weaving ride paralleling the swift McKenzie River across a covered bridge. Then the route ascends up and out of the Willamette Valley over the snow-covered Cascades. There are two ways to go: over the narrow, steep switchbacks of McKenzie Pass, which is almost always snowbound until late June, or the 20-mile longer, but somewhat easier, Santiam Pass which is about 500 feet less in elevation.

According to Dave Brown:

> The first of the major obstacles came three days into our trip. It seemed like the entire trip consisted of a series of hurdles anticipated with various degrees of fear, insecurity, and doubt. All required a high degree of mental preparation, and I believe as a group the obstacles were conquered much easier than if we had had to face the challenges all alone.

If you elect to ride over Santiam Pass, you will miss the lava fields which cover wide areas of the Three Sisters Wilderness. Full of dark rough rocks with little vegetation, these fields look like a barren and forboding planet.

In an earlier chapter, I explained why I chose to begin at this end of the trail. Those who rode westward were seeing the country in reverse order and, therefore, their perspectives were completely different. Although we are just beginning our "trip," there are those like Billy Steward who are riding their last days toward Reedsport:

> McKenzie Pass is the last pass before the coast. It's all downhill from here.

As you near the top, the road rounds a bend and comes out onto a lunar landscape of lava flows and broken rock, a field stretching off without grass or trees. And there is this panorama: Mt. Hood, Mt. Washington, Mt. Jefferson, and Three-Fingered Jack, showing their craggy peaks, some still covered with snow.

The blackberries of Oregon are the best. On our last day of riding, we picked a bucketful and rode to the nearest store, where we bought some real ice cream. Between six people, we devoured four half-gallons of ice cream, our last of many ice cream feasts and probably our best....

It was with mixed emotions that we rode our bikes into Reedsport, but once we rounded the bend in the road and went over the bridge, we came upon the sign of our aspirations: "Welcome to Reedsport, Oregon," the mystical city that we had talked of for so long. Just a port on a river that leads to the ocean, but paradise to us.

According to the Bikecentennial guidebook on McKenzie or Santiam Pass:

> Both passes have positive and negative features. If you have a choice (when both passes are open), base your decision on your cycling experience, how hard you want to work, and how much time you want to spend.

There are no services between McKenzie Bridge and Sisters. So when climbing either pass, make sure your supply of food is adequate for the next 40 miles or so.

During the early part of summer, snow and cold still linger in the Cascades and higher elevations. Especially during the nights, the temperature often drops below freezing. Dave Brown, who rode with one Trans-America group, relates:

> We were with a very experienced trip leader. One of the first things he asked us to do before leaving Reedsport was for us to set up all the tents. Then he checked each one, eliminating half of them. He reasoned that it was ridiculous for 12 people to carry 12 two-man tents. By doubling up, we not only cut our weight load, but we stayed warmer at night with two bodies generating heat.

The forest never seems to end. It is very green and lush due to the huge amounts of rainfall, or so it seems. I cannot think of a better time to be in Oregon than in springtime. The air is crisp and cool, and snow patches are hiding in the tree shadows. One trip diary reads: "From the Santiam snowfields, we coasted down the other side to rising temperatures of the desert." The Cascades' high peaks stop the rain from falling on their eastern slopes, making that side of Oregon a high plateau desert. This desert extends all along the Cascade range from Washington into northern California.

Not only is there a dramatic climate change, but the towns also show a different character. Many of them are empty shells of what once were booming mining towns. Towns in eastern Oregon are not like those found in the Willamette Valley. They are quite small, and many times several groups of bikers would outnumber the population. It seemed to many of them that Bikecentennial '76 was the biggest thing to happen to them in 100 years. Towns like Mitchell, Prineville, and Dayville are set in a brown land of sagebrush and juniper.

Riding between Sisters and John Day is to go through a land of gently rolling hills with only two difficult passes. But for every uphill, you are rewarded with the downhill. The last descent goes into Picture Gorge. The John Day River cut down through 15 or more basalt flows — each layer a different shade. Here, too, are found prehistoric pictographs over 5,000 years old.

This is the land of the cowboy, today more so even than Texas or Arizona. Cowboys reputedly placed great stock in their horses. I now know why. As you scan the road from horizon to horizon and see nothing but towering storm clouds, slanting rain, sage, and blowing dust, you realize that the next site of human habitation is 20 to 30 miles away, and the bike becomes every bit as important as the legendary cow pony. It is a remarkable machine.

Marshall Strickler, another biker, remembers:

> The route out of Mitchell starts up at once for seven miles. The terrain is arid, almost desert-like, and is best known as the

Painted Hills. It's the real oldtime West. Cowboys, miners, and I'm sure, dance hall girls, if you could find a dance hall. After the rather strenuous climb, there followed a l-o-n-g downhill ramble into Dayville for lunch. "Population 86." Truly the small town face of rural America.

It can never be said that Oregon is a boring place to ride. Just when you think you have flat land, another mountain pass appears. After John Day, there are several long, but easy, climbs toward Bates. An alternate route at this point includes about 18 miles of gravel, a couple more climbs but rewarding scenery, and the remains of gold mines and ghost towns. Drinking water through here is in short supply, so be sure that *both* water bottles are filled.

If you elect to stay on the main route and head for Baker, you will have good paved road but a climb, just the same, over Dooley Summit (5,392) with steep switchbacks on both sides of the mountain. Almost every climb in this land is complimented with, not only long coasting downhills, but beautiful views of distant mountains, rivers, and clear alpine lakes. If you pay attention to details, just east of Baker you will see the deep ruts that are still very evident of the famous Oregon Trail.

Halfway, located in the beautiful Pine Valley, is the last town in Oregon. It is a good place to rest and refill supplies before striking on for Hell's Canyon. For 18 miles you will parallel a canyon whose grandeur rivals that of the Grand Canyon of the Colorado. Although not as large in area, it is actually an average of 2,400 feet deeper than the Grand Canyon, making it the deepest gorge in North America. The Snake River, beginning in the Teton Range watershed, flows for 1,000 miles to the Columbia River. Its headwaters at the Columbia River confluence are gentle, but just 50 miles downstream it becomes a treacherous and dangerous river to the unaware. Early explorers quickly learned what the river had to offer, and many were drowned. This is the force which you can still see grinding away on the canyon walls.

Idaho, Home of Chief Joseph

After another hard climb out of Hell's Canyon over Brownlee Dam, there is the inevitable, delightful downhill. This one was designed for leisurely viewing of the scenery. Surrounded by mountains, you enter forested Idaho, the ancient land of the Nez Perce Indians.

White Bird Hill, often called the Hill of Idaho, has always, it seems, been a major obstacle. It was here in 1877 that General Perry and his army troops attacked Chief Joseph's band of Nez Perce; that skirmish was the beginning of the Nez Perce War and their attempt to escape to safety in Canada. For cyclists, it will be an unforgettable climb. With 13 switchbacks — eight and a half miles long and a seven degree grade — it was considered an engineering feat at its completion. In 1976, it was a pedaling feat for 4,000 cyclists. A new road now bypasses White Bird Hill, which means that traffic is almost nonexistent. They miss all the fun and the fantastic experience of navigating this road. The downhill, which is equally steep and challenging, is all yours to enjoy with few cars to get in your way.

Dave Brown relates:

> From the town of White Bird, we could see that awesome set of switchbacks going up the mountainside. Its top was hidden in ragged clouds. I felt like a link in a snake chain as each of our group began to ride up, swinging back and forth across the face of the mountain. You could look up and down and see riders on the various levels of switches slowly grinding their way upward. We could, in that small way, comprehend the struggle of the Nez Perce flight over the same route to Canada.
>
> Walking in the footsteps of Chief Joseph and his retreating band was an emotional experience. All along the route, after White Bird, markers told what specific historical events happened on that spot. Following the exact same route over mountain passes with the bicycle rather than with cars, our physical efforts were somewhat more comparable to their physical trauma, and something we could now relate to.

After Grangeville, Idaho, the largest town the trail goes through in Idaho, there is another steep descent into the forested hills which typify central Idaho. This is followed by an all too short one-day trip through the indescribable Lochsa River Valley, and according to Marshall Strickler:

> The road winds along the river through absolutely untarnished wilderness, no gas stations, no signs, no cafes, nothing, just river, multitudinous feeding creeks, the wilderness woods, and peaceful solitude. A perfect day.

From Kooskia to Lolo Hot Springs, the trail winds along the beautifully wild Lochsa River. Stands of lodgepole pines tower above, and cold water sparkles with white stars glancing over the river boulders. Until the Lewis and Clark Highway was completed in 1962, the Bitterroot range and surrrounding wilderness were largely the domain of the prospector and the backpacker. Fortunately, it is still a wild country. Uncommercialized, there are no services for the entire 80 mile distance. Having a choice between stores and motels or a national forest with cathedral-like giant pine trees, which would *you* choose?

9

The Rocky Mountains

There is a quiet splendor found in Montana, a magnificence felt when riding in the shadows of the snowcapped mountain peaks, a sense of awe and reverence when surrounded by the sky and space of this vast land.

By the time you reach Missoula, having crossed the coastal range and Cascades, the Rocky Mountains will sound exciting, but not formidable. There is nothing difficult about them with their long and gradual grades and maximum six percent climbs. You will find that the Appalachians are much more challenging.

Scenic Montana

It is difficult to say which of the sections or states are the most outstanding for scenery, but this part certainly ranks high. From Missoula, home office of Bikecentennial, you ride south with the Bitterroot range on your right for many miles. It is very rug-

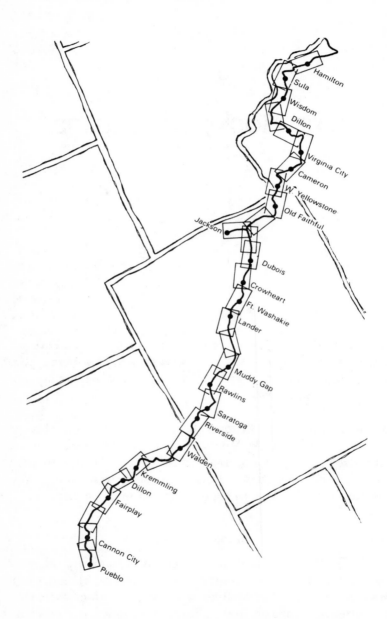

ged looking and snow covered most of the year. Melting snow forms innumerable streams meandering throughout the valley floor. It is a prosperous, peaceful Bitterroot Valley with rich-looking ranches and immaculate white frame houses in very small towns. Traffic is extremely light with only an occasional local car passing by. My journal notes: "The redwing blackbirds are making the cattails dance and sway. Kingfishers, meadowlarks, and barn swallows line the barbwire fence rows."

The ghosts of Lewis and Clark and Chief Joseph ride with you almost every day. For different reasons they made their way across this land when it was wild and, for Chief Joseph, not so peaceful — two men because they wanted to, and one because he was forced. All have left a piece of history and themselves on the mountain tops.

The mornings are quite cool, but the ascending sun warms the day. Traffic is almost nonexistent. The road climbs very gradually toward Sula, a two-building town, and the base of the twin passes, Lost Trail and Chief Joseph Pass, one mile beyond. Lost Trail was named by Lewis and Clark because for many days they were unable to find a route over these mountains. Today a good road climbs the seven or so miles over the top. It is a steady upward grade, but the views of distant tree-covered ridges and icy streams are breathtaking. Late spring flowers add splashes of yellow to the slopes. There are patches of snow on top of the Continental Divide — a 7,200-foot elevation. Eight more times the Continental Divide will be crossed before leaving the Rockies in Colorado.

From here it is all downhill into the beautiful Big Hole Valley. Jay Anderson went through Big Hole Battlefield on June 9, 1976, and noted in his journal:

> The morning has been cold, the west fork of the Bitterroot clear and wild, the gift of fresh-caught trout eagerly eaten before the the long haul over Lost Trail Pass and Chief Joseph Pass began. For days our group of 16 cyclists has crossed paths with Lewis and Clark who lost their way here trying to find the Bitterroot Valley, and with Nez Perce Indians, led by Joseph in their flight

from the U.S. Army toward the freedom of Canada. We pant and puff as we pedal our loaded ten-speeds up the seven miles of twisting grade where, perching on the Continental Divide, we enjoy our usual lunch of peanut butter and jelly sandwiches, cheese, and fruit. Washing this down with a squirt of now-warm river water from the ever-ready plastic bottle, we cruise down the Atlantic side of the Divide and into the Big Hole, a flat meadow ringed by mountains. The National Park Service's presentation on the battle at Big Hole, won by neither the Nez Perce nor the Army, plays no favorites. As the last slide dissolves on the screen, the curtains draw back to reveal the scene as it was: tepees standing innocently in the meadow, willows by the creek to cover a quietly approaching army.

I cannot hide a tear; Joseph has become one of my heroes, and not even the "Big Sky" of Montana is big enough to hold his words: "I will fight no more forever."

After Big Hole Battlefield, the valley opens up as if a giant hand had pulled the mountains away like a curtain from a window. It is a valley of small rolling knobs; streams are coursing everywhere amid sage and lush, green grass. The fields look like they have never been plowed — tens of thousands of acres. All around, on every horizon, there are snowcapped mountains, far, far away.

The silence continues: earth, sky and wind are suspended in the afternoon quiet. Riding into Wisdom, the town is so still the only thing I hear is the whisper of my tires. There isn't anything moving, neither person nor animal — nothing.

Openness and spacious skies continue to Jackson and Dillon. Forty-five miles between towns, and the cowboys love it. The summer winds are filled with the smell of cattle and sagebrush. Even the billowy clouds look like cows.

Twenty-two miles west of Dillon and four miles off the main road are the remains of the town of Bannack. Once a "rip, roaring" mining town when gold was discovered in the surrounding hills, it was also the first town in Montana and the first territorial capital. Like many of the towns of that era, it was one without any lawmakers or lawkeepers, and as a result, no one was punished for shooting another man. Naturally, Bannack became the gathering place for all the thieves and murderers, because there was a lot of gold to be stolen. All that remains of the town of 3,000 inhabitants is four buildings in various stages of weathering.

Just beyond Wisdom, there are about 11 miles of gravel. Between Jackson and Dillon, there are 45 miles with no services, no towns, nothing but space and sky and two mountain passes. Marshall Strickler said of this section: "Up and over the 7,400-foot pass after Jackson, which was the hardest pass to date due to stiff headwinds, plus altitude." These passes — Big Hole and Badger — neither of which is unusually steep, seem to plague eastbound cyclists with headwinds. Aside from these two climbs, the land is simply rolling country on and on into infinity.

Dillon is very western with its "whiskey row" and false front, tin facades dating back to 1888, Victorian houses, and a single hotel.

To move through this vast landscape is to rediscover the legends and lore of the West. The towns and attitudes are pretty much as they always were. After a while, you have become so accustomed to seeing this way of life that you begin to feel less like a tourist or traveler and more like you belong. Slowness is a wonderful equalizer. Your bicycle becomes your time machine and allows you the luxury of total appreciation of things surrounding you.

Gold was also discovered in the hills and valleys surrounding present-day town sites of Alder, Nevada City, and Virginia City. Miles of rockpiles line the road, the end result of dredging operations. The lure of wealth caused these greedy ones to mar the landscape even back then. Today the fortunes and most of the people are gone, and these ghostly towns make good movie settings for Hollywood. For example, *Little Big Man* was filmed in Virginia City. If you should blink while sitting in the funky Bale of Hay Saloon, you might just miss seeing Dustin Hoffman disappear out the swinging doors.

Over high mountains, down into long valleys — this seems to

be the pattern in Montana. All who rode out from Virginia City can tell you about that day. Although the climb is only three miles long, the grade is seven percent at times. Add a very strong headwind, and you can hardly *walk* against forces like that. But the best is ahead of you. From the top, take time to look about before racing down to Ennis. You can see to infinity, and words like "grandeur" and "majestic" come to mind. Mountains disappear into mist, and the valley sparkles in morning sunlight. You will long remember your downhill. It is fast and fun, curving and carefree for 11 miles! Your average speed is probably 50 mph. Welcome to Ennis.

Gradually the landscape changes to something resembling alpine. Pine forests become more noticeable, and the mountains are closing in again. Streams have widened, and you ride along the shores of Hebgen Lake. Ahead is Yellowstone and the magnificent Tetons; behind the still evident scars remain from the 1959 earthquake which buried alive at least 28 campers. A visitor center explains the terrible details of that fateful night.

Yellowstone and the Tetons

At first light of day, we enter Yellowstone Park and race in and out of the cool tree shadows, while the cumbersome campers and aluminum foil wombs are still clustered around the blackened circle of last night's bonfire.

My journal recalls:

> I see something like Old Faithful — and all the smaller vapor puffs rising white against the morning sky with the smell of sulphur heavy in the air — and I wonder what it was like to be the first one to see these things instead of the millionth person this summer.

Yellowstone is a great place to visit, but it is a better place to leave quickly. The people make it unreal; there are too many of them and the roads can no longer accommodate the traffic. You must make your escape as early in the morning as possible, and somehow the beauty is diminished by all the metal-encapsulated humanity.

What would John Colter say if he could see "his" country now? He was probably the first white man to see the hydrothermal wonders, or at least the first to admit to the phenomenon. The newspapers figured he was slightly crazy and, rather than believe him, they loved to poke fun at him and his stories.

The Tetons have a silent beauty reflected in Jackson Lake. Again, the ubiquitous tourists somehow come between you and the mountains. Only by seeking out the primitive paths can you get away from the commercial madness.

Yellowstone and the Grand Tetons are the only national parks through which the current Trans-America Trail passes, and this is probably a very good thing. Until the national parks begin to place restrictions on motorized traffic within their boundaries, there is little room for the bicyclist to enjoy a safe and carefree trip through them. For that matter, I wonder how many of the motorists truly enjoy driving through them. Those with campers are under additional pressures; since time restrictions exist in the campgrounds, campers seem to race from one campsite to the next one, hoping there will be room for them when they arrive. Therefore, these campers really cannot, and do not, take the time along the way to see the sights which they drove all that distance to see in the first place.

To "rediscover America" is one of the reasons for this bike trail. To me, that also means meeting its people. For some strange reason, people act differently when they are not in familiar surroundings. A new set of rules and rituals takes over, and people cease being people and become *tourists*. The sad thing is that not many people can handle the "rules." It takes years of practice in order to achieve the status and grace of a person who evolves from a *tourist* to a *person who travels*. Meanwhile, Yellowstone, the Tetons, and the town of Jackson have their share of tourists.

I recorded the following in my journal:

It is the middle of June, and a snowstorm during the night has laid down a fresh mantle of white to the 5,000-foot level. The sky is filled with another set of approaching storm clouds. To the east is the mountain we plan to conquer in our "escape" from this most beautiful of all valleys. The reports of ice and snow on Togwotee only serve to increase our apprehensions about riding to the next planned stop, the town of Dubois. We throw sanity to the winds and bid our goodbyes to old man Teton.

There were a fair number of cyclists whose experience and general comment about the weather over Togwotee Pass was "appalling!" Actually, Togwotee is not a bad climb, because there are several level spots and downs to allow for second winds. In all, there are about ten miles of uphill climbing; but when the weather moves into snow conditions, Togwotee is "misery hill."

The journal of Marshall Strickler relates:

> Sleet, snow, rain. Wow! We started at about a 6,000-foot elevation. The climb took four hours of steady pushing. After the first half hour, it started raining, which quickly changed to snow pellets. The steady wind drove these into our faces and eyes, reducing visibility and making breathing even more difficult. The snow started sticking. Visibility dropped to zero. Previous tire tracks disappeared in minutes. On and on and on. No end to it. Our hands and feet are numb. Compensations — no sunburn here. Finally the top! The downhill, 13 miles, was cold but a pleasure. The snow stopped, and it was just cold rain. We hit a friendly ranch-restaurant, and it was just like a ski lodge, with a large fireplace, open on two sides with everyone's wet socks, shoes, and raingear steaming as 30 cyclists tried to thaw out. We ate everything in sight and exchanged horror stories about the Togwotee climb. Ah, the joys of summer cycling.

At Togwotee's 9,000-foot top, winter still raged. Summer returned after 7,000 feet, and the remaining 14 downhill miles were warm, sunny, and dry. With the wind at your back and the sun casting long shadows, what else could you ask for?

The Wind River Reservation waits on the other side. The entire topography has changed dramatically. It is truly amazing how a mountain can affect the land. Red sandstone formations are found on the left side of the road, whereas there are green rolling hills, like the Connecticut Valley, on the right side — a real study in contrasts. Can the Wyoming Badlands be far ahead?

My journal reads:

> The Wyoming Basin. It is a barren landscape with unbroken horizons and where strong winds prevail. There are red cliffs like Arizona and layered hills like Texas and New Mexico. There is rolling desert, and hard land with sage and some cactus. According to the guidebooks, it is a hot, dry area. Other people who have traveled this way claim this is the most difficult desert area for survival in the country. It was raining and cold all the time I was there! Odors of alfalfa and clover were all along the way, and in profusion, lining the highway, a weed with delicate yellow, white, or purple flowers.

Still the land of the cowboy and the cattle drive, it is not unusual to get caught up in the midst of a cattle drive, since they are a common occurrence out here.

Buffalo once roamed these grasslands, and antelopes still play. You do not have to look far to see them; alone or in herds of 20 or more, they stare back at you. Like the antelopes, the biker is trying to cope and adapt to this environment. For the antelopes, it is their land. To the biker, it is a dry, barren land of nothingness — no water, a few low trees, and lots of rocks. How insignificant each individual feels, even knowing that they are very much a part of the land. It is a time for each biker to reflect upon the interaction between the land and himself.

Jade fields are here and a petrified forest is near Dubois. The graves of Chief Washakie and Sacajawea, both friends of the white man, can be found south of Dubois. In 1865, when the Crow, Cheyenne, and Sioux decided to do away with the white settlers, Washakie helped the army; and Sacajawea guided the Lewis and Clark expedition through the area.

Between Lander and Rawlings, there are a couple of very small towns, more like truck stops. To me, this is a land to make one really feel alone, as if you are the only person in the world. Every so often one sees a dirt road wandering away toward the hills; two of these are the remains of the Oregon Trail and the Pony Express route. For miles, this desolation continues — with only rolling hills for company. Over the Beaver Divide, the biker only finds an even higher plain. There is nothing but flat terrain through the Sweetwater Valley.

Beyond Rawlings, there are a couple of very small, western flavor, ex-mining towns which are separated by fierce cross-winds. The prevailing winds are westerly, and they do blow, and bikers riding in either direction find themselves canted over at least ten degrees to counteract these forces. After a while, the wind begins to get on your nerves, and all you want to do is get somewhere, anywhere, out of the wind.

This wind was in our favor, however, when we took a side trip up to Medicine Bow, a snowcapped mountain all by itself surrounded by the barren desert. With the wind at our backs, it blew us into the higher elevations of trees and green, lush meadows, snow patches, and beaver ponds.

I recorded the following description in my journal:

> Since leaving Rawlings, we have been following the North Platt River Valley. Just north of Saratoga, we cross the Overland Trail dating back to the 1850s, a rutted, dirt track leading off into the bleak, barren nowhere. We almost thought we saw the dust as the ghostly stage dropped down over the ridge. We could begin to understand how the huge wind wagons of bygone times would be the practical thing to have.

The town of Encampment has several claims to fame. In 1851 it was the site of the famous fur trapper's rendezvous, and in the late 1890s, it became a mining town when copper was discovered nearby. Today, you can see a section of the town that has been restored, complete with mining buckets, overhead tramways, and miscellaneous artifacts.

Rocky Mountain High

What Wyoming is, Colorado is not. You can tell when you have crossed into Colorado even without seeing the stateline sign. Suddenly you see less sage and more grass and aspen, and the hills somehow look different too. The abundance of green is very restful on the eyes and mind after the days of sere, brown countryside.

North Park is the first of four basins which the Trail traverses before descending into the plains east of Pueblo, Colorado. The North Platte River flows through this beautiful valley, complete with grassy meadows rimmed by pine trees and snow covered mountains. Prosperous ranches of thousands of acres are the only signs of "development." The side winds of Wyoming are now the tail winds of Colorado, and the terrain becomes more rolling. Fast runs downhill past wild and wide, lonely, windswept vistas make the biker feel like an earthbound eagle who soars on wings of wheels.

The average altitude in Colorado is 6,800 feet, making it the highest state in the country. The average cyclist may experience some slight discomfort for a few days until the body has become acclimatized. But if you have been riding the Trail all along, you should already be used to the altitude, having been at the higher elevations throughout Wyoming, Montana, and Idaho. As the route continues south, it becomes more hilly. Each day takes us deeper into the heart of the Rockies. Colorado would have to be considered the Rocky Mountain state.

Without too much puffing and panting, we climbed over the 7,000-foot Muddy Pass with the rabbit ears rock formation following our progress. Once on top, we had our lunch in the cool shade of the aspen trees. From here our climbing was rewarded with several long downhills into Kremmling. This was followed by a long 55-mile or so uphill run into Breckenridge, the posh ski resort community. This is a good place to celebrate in some way the sense of achievement of having made it to the 9,000-foot elevation. Just ahead is the Hoosier Pass. Although Hoosier is the highest point on the Trail at 11,541 feet, it is not as difficult as you might think, just challenging. Since you are already at more than 9,000 feet, the distance to the top is only 2,500 feet more, over a ten mile distance. Nevertheless, everyone will pant and puff in triple time, and legs will feel like lead because the air is so thin.

The following description is found in my journal:

> Once on top we were overcome by the indescribable feeling of success. Bikers stood around in small groups with that silly self-satisfied grin and flushed with a great feeling of triumph. Cheers went out to each straggler as he or she appeared from around the final switchback. All drank in the view at the top of the world. What is there to be said when you are at eye level with the surrounding mountain peaks?
>
> It was a *Sound of Music* background for our victory lunch above the treeline. Leaving our bikes leaning against the sign, we hiked up to a grassy meadow covered with many varieties of wild, alpine flowers and lichen-spotted rocks. Several hundred feet below was a clear, blue, mountain lake. Waterfalls were rushing down the opposite mountainsides from snowfields. A cold, clear stream was a few feet away from us and just before the edge of "our" meadow, where it fell away to the lake, one single bristlecone pine tree was clinging to a rock pile. Its branches were like long, golden curls. From every angle the tree was a handsome, windblown sculpture.
>
> After lunch we hiked farther up the slope to the remains of a mining operation where a few weathered shacks were tenaciously hanging on. The main mine shaft was still blocked with snow, and a smashed ore bucket was in a rusty heap among the boulders. A storm was moving and forming far to the west, and giant thunderheads were building their way over the mountains. Down in the valley the town of Alma was in sunlight, and we raced the gathering storm from off the mountain top.

Alma is six miles down, and we arrived in the center of town in only nine minutes! The first cars to pass us were snow covered. Another 17 minutes and we were in Fairplay, seven miles farther. That's what we call downhill riding.

The Fairplay Hotel where we stayed the night was a step back in time. What a delight it was to find a place, single and unique, that is not part of the repetitious motel chains where each room has been stamped out from the same chrome and plastic mold. When the Fairplay Hotel was built, the blight of planned obsolescence was not even known. Its lobby with dark wooden walls and carved pillars welcomes you into another world, and the bannister running along the open staircase shows the wear of the many hands of travelers and time.

On the edge of town is another restored mining town called South Park, where many of the buildings are still sitting on their original foundations. There are a total of 29 buildings, and they are an excellent example of a typical Colorado mining town during the late 1800s.

According to the Bikecentennial guidebook, "After Hartsel, there are no services and no water available for the next 50 miles." But, there is a town called Guffy hiding at the end of a dusty road in among the hills. It is a ghost town in the making, or maybe it is just a town time forgot. At one time there were 2,000 people living here, but nothing is left now except a few wooden buildings with false fronts, sagging porches, and boarded-up windows. It gives one an eerie feeling to wander amid the dusty streets and see a town having the last dying twitches. One cannot help but wonder where all the people went and what they would say if they could see their town now. Only two houses had running water, and a number did not have electricity. I have never before been in a town that is neither ghost nor real, but without a doubt, this was a fascinating place.

Beside the few remaining houses, there is only one commercial building still active — the general store. Inside, a potbelly stove — the center of interest — was ringed by chairs. Shelves against the walls have only a few dust-covered basic items, all smelling with age. The sun finally sets in quiet timelessness over Guffy, but tomorrow will be soon enough for us to return to the present.

For contrast, Royal Gorge is a few miles farther along the road. If highly commercialized playgrounds are your bag, then you can forget Guffy in preference to here. Royal Gorge claims to have the highest automobile suspension bridge in the world, but all it does is connect two parking lots. It should be converted into a footbridge. Better still, it should not have been built in the first place. Imagine a car packed with humanity, kids three deep in the back seat among the pillows and luggage trying to get a look into the gorge. The posted speed limit is 10 mph. Someone aims a Polaroid out the window. Snap! and they have the whole scene recorded for posterity. When they get home, they will probably have trouble remembering what that blurred image was.

The land is beginning another transition that informs you that you are leaving the mountains behind at last. From here, the route is almost all downhill into the Colorado plains and Kansas. My journal records: "I am going to miss the high, wild craggy peaks and streams, the alpine flowers, and rocky strewn grassy meadows."

Billy Stewart IV, who rode from east to west, made the following observations about the Colorado Piedmont area:

> Eastern and western Colorado are so different it's amazing. Eastern is very arid, and I didn't see any major farming. The land is barely green; only scrub grass grows in the sandy soil. the only grazing animals I saw were horses, and they were few and far between. The land is as flat as Kansas, with the mountains rising abruptly out of the plains. You can see the Rockies two days' ride away.

Squatting at the base of the mountains is Pueblo, the largest town through which the Trans-America Trail passes. This is the halfway point in miles — 2,125 in both directions, and something like the point of no return. This also marks the division of the seasons — from now on, it is guaranteed to be summer. You can send your woolies and underwear home from the Pueblo Post Office.

The most amazing thing to me about this town of Pueblo is the way in which they prepared for July 4, 1976, the day we pedaled into their city. They did nothing! Even though we made a number of inquiries as to what was happening, no one really seemed to know or care. And that was sad.

10

The Plains and the Ozarks

The highway hangs in the heat waves and haze like a tightwire strung between two grain elevator pylons. Pedaling toward the rising round towers on the horizon, my cadence is measured by the lonely Kansas wind.

The only way we could tell where eastern Colorado ended and Kansas began was by a sign — "Welcome Bikers to Friendly Kansas." There was nothing around us but an endless land of sagebrush, rolling hills, and ranches. Towns are few and far between and seem to rise from nowhere in the middle of endless fields.

In Brandon, Colorado, a small town alongside the inevitable, ubiquitous grain elevator and railroad track, was a tiny general store covered with flaking, wrinkled paint. An "Eat Wonder Bread" push strip sign was holding a rusty screen door together. Run by two older people, this old, old building stood on a dusty sidestreet. It was cool and dark inside, and there were only a couple of rows of half-empty shelves, and a squatty pop cooler was near the door. The whole scene was probably the same in 1950 or 1940. There was nothing different or added, just aging in the sunblown prairie. Across the street were the remains of the hardware store. "When did he go out of business?" "Oh, sometime around the end of the war, I think." He was referring to 1945, and the showcases were still in evidence along with a few remaining dry and dusty goods.

The Journey Across Kansas

My journal notes:

> The land is either gently rolling or flat. You can see a hundred miles to where the grass falls off the edge of the world. Roads are straight, straight, straight. Not a bend, not a curve.

About the only thing you can say to describe western Kansas is that it goes on and on and on. These high plains are hot and dry, as the Rockies do not allow more than 12 or so inches of rain annually to fall on this side of them.

When there is any variance in the landscape, Kansas makes it a state park, as in the case of El Quartelijo. A ridge of land north of Scott City with rock outcroppings, a river, and cottonwood trees, has the remains of the only known Indian pueblo in Kansas. In 1898 the remains of a seven-room structure which dated back to the 1600s were uncovered. They are believed to be from the Taos Indian culture.

Roads in Kansas are usually in very good condition and are only lightly traveled. The big, unpleasant problem is the ceaseless wind. Someone once asked an oldtimer: "Does the wind always blow like this?" "No," he replied. "Sometimes it blows from the other direction." There are no natural barriers to stop the wind or the storms; they come from any compass direction. The settlers of the 1930s learned that lesson the hard way.

According to the Bikecentennial guidebook, they:

> plowed up the sod and allowed it to dry to a brick-like surface. Destroying the deep grass roots was a terrible error on the plains where the wind blows almost constantly. Wherever the soil was dried by drought, the wind would pick up the dust and carry it for long distances.

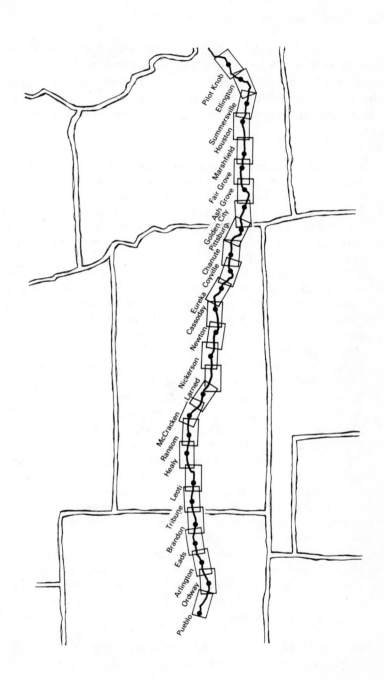

Pilot Knob
Ellington
Summersville
Houston
Marshfield
Fair Grove
Ash Grove
Golden City
Pittsburg
Chanute
Coyville
Eureka
Cassoday
Newton
Nickerson
Larned
McCracken
Ransom
Healy
Leoti
Tribune
Brandon
Eads
Arlington
Ordway
Pueblo

Across the distant fields, the skeleton remains of many of the Dust Bowl farms were weathering with time, and we passed many an abandoned windmill. These farmers certainly gave John Steinbeck something to write about.

Marshall Strickler, riding eastward, had this to say about Kansas:

> June 23: Tribune. Weather: absolutely perfect. Cool, overcast until about 10:00, then bright, warm, gentle winds quartering on the tail mostly. The day ended with a typical Kansas thunder-bumper, complete with intermittent hail and great gouts of water. The weather seems to play an inordinately important part of each day. It has a great impact on the enjoyment of each day's tour.
>
> Roads are section-line straight in Kansas, running north and south or east and west. Never diagonally. Again, the bit about "amber waves of grain" was never more true than here in Kansas.
>
> Never saw such hospitality. The innkeeper and his wife at Tribune cranked up a batch of ice cream for us. Somebody picked up the tab for dinner!
>
> June 24: Weather, magnificent. How can I embellish this day? What superlatives are fitting? The endless, unfenced fields, so refreshing a change from Colorado and Wyoming where everything in sight is fenced with stern admonitions of "no trespassing." The noisy silence of it all, silence until you become aware of incessant bird calls, the chirping crickets, even the scratching of the turtles' toenails as they march slowly and majesticaly across the highways, the slow, steady "chuf-chuf-chuf" of the oil well pump engines muttering to themselves like giant hearts. And every once in a while the mosquito-like whine of the itinerant crop duster plying his trade on the horizon. All part of the majestic awe and inspiration of Kansas. Unending grain, oil, cattle, silos, and elevators, and quiet, soft-spoken, pleasant people. Kansas, a blessed place with an inspiring four square beauty all its own; it is every bit as impressive as the Rockies, in an entirely different way. Today was truly a fine, fine day. I'll not soon forget this great day in Kansas.

This is our land. The wheated prairie undulates like gigantic waves from the prehistoric sea. We sail on, pedals spinning in

the dancing sunlight. Biking across Kansas can also become tedious, and many cyclists have unglamorous and even unkind re-
marks to make about the land. In a very short while you will
even find it hard, with any clarity, to separate one day from another because not much change takes place mile after mile.

One Dutch cyclist remarked: "When you ride in Kansas, you
don't miss the mountains because the people are so fine."

But the people who live there are unlike any other. Their
kindness will be recalled by every cyclist during the quiet mo-
ments with that faraway smile born of fond memories which
grow better with each passing year. The related experiences told
by every biker who crossed the state are without end. It is hard
to imagine anyone not having had something good happen to
them here.

Linda Robbins relates the following story:

> Every flat tire in Kansas brought offers of rides to the nearest
> town. After spending most of one day trying to wait out the 108
> degree heat, we made a run for Eureka and ended up riding on a
> busy highway in the dark. The Eureka police, hearing about us
> from truck drivers on citizen band radios, sent trucks out to bring
> us into town. After depositing us at the city park, they told us a
> locked fence surrounded the swimming pool, but said that no
> one would notice if we quietly climbed over it.
>
> One Kansas woman even patrolled the highway looking for rid-
> ers, leading them to the family farm for ice cream, iced tea, and a
> guided tour of the grain elevator. I left Kansas with a great love
> for its warm, open people.

Just passing you on the highway, either coming or going, everybody waved, and I mean everybody unless it was a vehicle
with out-of-state plates. I never knew there were so many different ways to wave, from broad ones accompanied by equally
broad grins to the tiny index finger salute. The best of all were
the ones which required several steps. Remember, it is hot out
there, and many cars are air-conditioned these days. A window
is never open to the summer breezes anymore. So, in order to
wave, first the window is rolled down just far enough to stick

four fingers out to the second knuckle. Braver ones would stick out their entire hand as far as the wrist, then wiggle furiously. The horn is tapped, "beep, beep," and as soon as the waver was sure you saw the greeting, the fingers were quickly withdrawn. Hurry! close the window. And the car speeds on ahead.

Camping is no problem as throughout Kansas you are allowed to use the many roadside rest areas. Food and water can become a problem, however. When you do find a grocery store, stock up. It is not unusual to go 35, 40, or even 50 miles between larders. Although the towns listed on the map are somewhat closer than this, many of them no longer support any type of cafe or food center. This is where the Bikecentennial map is invaluable because it tells you which towns do have stores, unless they too have closed since the map's printing.

After Newton, things begin to look different. The land is greener, more trees appear, and there is more rolling country. Is this a prelude to Missouri, perhaps?

Recorded in my journal, I find:

> There are lots of wild flowers all along the roadway. Black-eyed susans, small daisies, clover, sweet-peas. There were trumpet vines climbing over weathered tree stumps. A bobwhite was calling across the meadow while I stopped to pick a wild stalk of daisy blossoms.

The Missouri Ozarks

What Kansas is, the Missouri Ozarks are not. The hills begin gradually and gently enough, and at first they are fun. With the fast downhills and steep, but short, uphills, it is good-bye flat land.

Early morning, just before dawn, is the best time to ride. This is when the green hills are shrouded in their sleepy layer of haze and ground mist, and leaves sparkle with diamonds of dew. Many streams crisscross the countryside, and if you pay attention, you can find watercress. Mix it with oil, vinegar, chopped onion, salt, and it is delicious!

The farther east you go, the higher the humidity becomes. As long as you are moving through the air, you do not notice it. But if you stop and stand in the same spot for 30 seconds, you will be standing in a wet puddle.

The Jack's Fork River flows through Alley Springs, and for a change one should try a canoe trip down this beautiful refreshing waterway. Oak and maple trees, interspersed with sheer limestone walls, line the river banks, and there are cool, deep holes for impromptu swims.

At the general store just over the bridge, we reserved our canoes, left our bikes in the back storeroom, and headed downriver to Eminence. Our bikes were delivered to us on schedule at the bridge in exchange for the canoes, which gave us a thrilling and invigorating five miles of river adventure.

Each day the hills are more intimidating; their steepness and repetition seem endless until they show you their all-out effort between Eminence and Ellington. Marshall Strickler wrote:

> I have never seen such hills. The Rockies were pikers compared to these hills in Missouri. You leave the town of Eminence, and the road goes straight up and up. The grade is next to impossible. Many riders were beaten by the end of the day. You wish you were back in flat Kansas.

And from my own journal:

> I do believe the road between Eminence and Ellington is the "twistiest" and steepest road we will ever ride over. What a stretch! Any hill from now on can only seem mild and easy compared to these. Even so, there were 26 beautiful miles with forest on either side of the road. Early morning cool light was filtering through the hazy dawn. Every so often a clearing would open up for a brief glimpse across fields of corn, and then the maples and oaks would move in close again. There isn't a man-made roller-coaster anywhere in the world to equal the pleasure, thrill, and agony of these hills.

Unlike Kansas people, Missourians are friendly but conservative. Their neat, little houses and well-tended gardens reflect their desire for semi-isolation. Linda Robbins recorded the following in her journal:

> The finest thing about Missouri was its old people. In every town we found old men who spent their days sitting on curbs, chewing tobacco, and talking. The slow-paced life was, as Randy a southern Californian said, "Sort of like a midwestern Haight-Ashbury."

Modern lifestyles are accepted much more slowly by these hillfolks. Rather, they have a deep pride in the things they make with their hands. And again, Linda Robbins relates:

> In Walnut Grove, Missouri, "population 442," I learned that with a little oldtime ingenuity, just about any place can become a bike shop — even the local feed and grain store. A bolt from my front derailleur broke near the town and made it impossible to shift. There was no bike shop, so I asked an old man sitting on the curb if there was a hardware store nearby. "Not exactly a hardware store," he drawled, "but y'all might find something at the feed and grain store down the street."
> I entered the wood-frame building with some skepticism and found five men, all dressed in overalls.
> "Hep ya?" asked one.
> I explained my problem and the men shuffled out to loook over my bike. One man drilled a hole through a steel rod, so it could be used as a spacer for the broken derailleur. While that was being done, another went home and brought back a plate of cookies.
> After considerable time and testing, the component had been repaired and I was ready to go, having pleaded unsuccessfully to be allowed to pay for the work. I rode away, hearing a now-familiar phrase, "Y'all be careful now, y'hear?"

Interestingly enough, the Ozarks' hills and hollows are the only large area of rugged topography encountered between the Rockies and the Appalachian Mountains. After Farmington, the hills finally gave way to rolling foothills all the way to the Mississippi River and the French town of Ste. Genevieve.

Ste. Genevieve, the oldest permanent settlement west of the Mississippi, dates back to 1725 when Missouri was yet a part of the French territory. Many of the buildings are original eighteenth and nineteenth century structures. Others are old brick homes, and one in particular — the Price Brick House — is believed to be the oldest brick house west of the Mississippi River. Where the first American court once convened, there is now a tavern and restaurant.

My own journal records:

> Ducking into its cool interior was a step into a forgotten era. The room smelled of a thousand wood fires, old pipes smoked during relaxed conversation. What a relief from the white glare of the summer sun and heat. Several cold beers later it was possible to drag a body out to tour the rest of this miniature New Orleans, with a silent promise to return to the Brick House for a delicious fish dinner.

The Big Muddy and three more states separate you from Yorktown.

11

Bluegrass

Trip rhythm: The regularity of time and distance, an absolute order of so many pedal strokes pulling the sun along.

Stretching out in front of you is the great Mississippi River whose crossing is made possible by a small, anachronistic, somewhat rickety ferry. Sometimes it runs; sometimes it does not. There simply is little need of a schedule for this old-timer. Bridges farther down the river carry most of the motor traffic now. The ferry chugs its way along the levee, and at last you push your bicycle onto the shores of southern Illinois. For a very brief span of time, you had been riding the waves of an almost forgotten time — that of the riverboat men.

Entering the Land of Lincoln

Uphill and on to Carbondale. The terrain, similar to eastern Missouri, continues on this side of the river with hills and bluffs hiding fields of corn, lakes, and forested hollows. It is the same stone bluff country which continues all across the state; at the opposite edge, river pirate lore comes alive at Cave-in-Rock State Park which, except for mosquitoes, is a great place to camp.

From high bluffs you can see the heavy mist rising off the Ohio River, blurring the Kentucky forests on the opposite bank. The tall grass is soaked with morning dew, and everything feels very moist, humid, and sticky.

Down by the water's edge is the cave; a 25-foot entrance lures you into its enormous interior. Indians once used it as a council

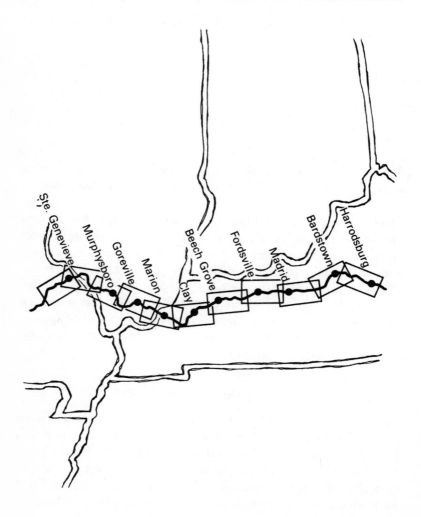

meeting chamber and left their writings on the walls, which have all but been obliterated by the modern scribbling Kilroys. It became a landmark to the riverboat men and the settlers making their way along the river. By the early 1800s, it became a source of treachery. River pirates would ambush cargo-loaded rafts from the cave, kill the occupants and, of course, steal the goods. Its last claim to fame was that of a bar, gambling casino, and whorehouse known as the Liquor Vault and later The Cave-Inn. Pirates continued to frequent the cave and even printed counterfeit money. After they were finally eliminated, the cave stood idle for almost 100 years before the state of Illinois changed the name to Cave-in-Rock and made it a state park.

Illinois can be a two-day state or a three-day or even a four-day state. It depends how much you enjoy riding over gravel roads, and there are 31 miles of gravel broken into several stretches between Carbondale and the Ohio River. I made it a two-dayer.

It was in Illinois where I really felt like an unseen alien just passing over the land. The nearer one gets to the east coast, the ''busier'' the people become, the less they see you, and the less they are inclined to talk to you, ask questions, or go out of their way to display any sign of friendliness. It is a shame because their part of the country is so beautiful.

All day long we rode over gently rolling hills and passed by green fields, corn fields, and fruit farms. We saw the land and tried to see the people, but they did not really see us. There was one exception, in Elizabeth Town. It seemed as if all the friendly people were fighting the heat and humidity in the cool interior of the Bate Mann Tavern. No one would let us pick up our beer tab, and the bartender sent out for orders of spareribs and insisted we eat something. Another man made certain that we had a place to stay for the night. They renewed our belief that friendly people do live in southern Illinois.

I noted in my journal:

Each day the land is closing in. There are no more 100-mile vistas, no more long, straight stretches of road, or the excitement of long, mountainous downhills. The trees are tight against the road as it curves and dips into patterns of hills and hollows, and the towns are much closer together. Population density is increasing although these backroads are still very much backwoods country.

Bluegrass Country

At Cave-in-Rock on another ferry, more modern this time, we crossed the Ohio River into Kentucky and the sights and sounds of Bluegrass country.

It seems almost without exception that each state had two distinctly different halves. The rain-forested pine country in western Oregon is in contrast to its eastern high plain desert; and the alpine territory of western Colorado changes to the Great Plains, high and dry. Each western half is in contrast to the eastern sector. This sharp contrast likewise continues in Kentucky.

Western Kentucky is beautiful bicycling country. There is variety and something clean and wholesome about the rich farms and well-kept homes surrounded by grassy fields and forests. The tree shadows trace cool patches across the roads and the rolling hills in western Kentucky are similar to those of Missouri in scenery only. Traffic is light, but the Appalachians are just ahead.

The shortest of all five sections of the trail, this is one of the most pleasant rides. It is also very historic, and it is here that you begin to get a feel for westward expansion and early colonization. Folklore abounds in the names of Daniel Boone, James Harrod and George Rogers Clark, Stephen Foster, and, of course, Abe Lincoln.

It was Boone who established the Wilderness Trail, and Clark was instrumental in winning Kentucky away from the British during the Revolutionary War. There is Old Fort Harrod in Harrodsburg, the oldest white settlement in Kentucky. In fact, Captain James Harrod arrived in the area before Boone, but for some unknown reason his exploits were never legend. Perhaps Boone just had a better public relations department, because they both took the same risks in reaching this new land.

Also in Harrodsburg something of the Old South still manages to come through. The dignity and grace of a time when life was opulent and tranquil is found at a place called Beaumont Inn. Wandering around the grounds or sitting on the pillared porch brings visions of long, lacy skirts, formal dress, and mint juleps. Once a very exclusive girl's school, the Inn is still furnished with original pre-Civil War furnishings.

Near Hodgenville stands the historic site of Abraham Lincoln's birth. The cabin which is thought to be his birthplace is entombed by a marble and granite memorial building. I say "thought to be" because they are not certain that this is the same cabin, since the original home was moved to several different locations, and with each move some of the logs were destroyed and replaced.

Called Sinking Spring Farm, the family lived here only two and a half years before moving several miles north to Knob Creek Farm. An oak tree which was over 100 years old when Lincoln was born still stands on the edge of the land. Certainly Abe Lincoln played at its broad base.

Throughout all of western Kentucky, food and lodging is easy to come by. However, every Bikecentennial rider will long remember the Falls of Rough — some with love, others with not much love, depending upon their values and attitudes or how well the day had gone up to that point. The Rough River was the site of one of the first paddle-driven lumber mills in the country. There was also a grain mill which has survived the ravages of weather and time. Named Green Mill, it was built by the Green family in 1823 and was operated by them until 1963, or 140 years! It overlooked a pretty river lined with limestone walls and dense green trees.

What remained of a storage shed on the far side of the river was a designated Bike Inn. It contained a cast-iron potbelly stove, a 50-gallon drum full of drinking water, and a bulletin board stating, among other things, that the nearest food store was three miles away. One side of the block building was open to the river and all the world, and a few army cots took up the remainder of the dusty floor space. Like I said, it was either love or hate at first sight.

Here, too, one is becoming more and more aware of the two
major conflicts — the Civil War and the Revolutionary War.
The Civil War plays a more prominent part in Kentucky history
and well it should. A short ten miles south of Harrodsburg and
the Trans-America Trail is the site of the climax of Kentucky's
Civil War battles — the Battle of Perryville. This was the blood-
iest battle in Kentucky, although it lasted only four short hours;
during that afternoon in October 1861, 7,000 people died. And
this in the state whose citizens did not want to have any part in
the conflict.

Kentucky is a state of contradictions. There are religious
groups who preach abstinence and have succeeded in making almost all but one or two counties dry counties. And yet the hills
are full of distilleries making moonshine bourbon, and the major crop is that "filthy weed," tobacco. Standing in the middle
of almost every tobacco field is the dark weathered barn, distinc-
tive in design, waiting for the season's crop ripening at its base.
Mile after mile, the broad-leafed tobacco plants flourished between the hills and "hollers." Off and away a tiny cabin would
stand with its back against the hazy green hillsides.

Marshall Strickler called the country a "gigantic park." The
most apt word to describe Kentucky is "pleasant," and so it was
with the early settlers. Pleasant Ridge, Pleasant Valley, Pleasant-
ville, Pleasant Acres, and so on, leap at you from every crossroad
sign. This is, I suppose, because the land — soft, rounded, and
vastly fertile — was a wonderland for tired settlers who were
worn out from crossing the Appalachians.

Berea is the Appalachian gateway and home of Berea College.
On the campus you will find one of the best collections of Appalachian art, homecrafts, books and musical instruments, as
well as bluegrass music at its finest. According to our guidebook, this mountain school is "devoted to the preservation of
Appalachian culture and the heritage of the mountain people."
However, I wonder how many cyclists in 1976 were able to get
past the litter and trash to appreciate the culture they were supposed to find beyond Berea.

12

The Appalachians

To experience beauty as well as ugliness makes for a total balance of perspective. How well could beauty be appreciated if that was all there would be to life's experiences?

The Face of Eastern Kentucky

The Appalachians — eastern Kentucky — how can this half still be called Kentucky? Judging from the opinions of most of the cyclists with whom I have talked, this section of the trail is not remembered with much fondness. It is not that the scenery suddenly vanished, but it is what the inhabitants did to mar their part of the state. And perhaps, we are all to blame in some way for allowing this to continue happening. "They just don't care" is an oft heard reason or excuse. It certainly is an easy one to grab onto and an easy way in which to turn our backs on the problem. Who knows what the solutions are? But the fact remains that eastern Kentucky is a mess. It seems that the common denominator for trash tossers is poverty. At least in this country it appears to be true. Look around at any city. Where is the filth? It is certainly not at the rich man's front door! Could this be the beginning of finding the solution?

What else is there to say about this part of the Trans-America Trail? The main purpose of the trail is to show you the faces of America — to help you rediscover your country. That would include all of it, the good along with the bad. Until now all the cyclist has seen is beauty — clean, small towns, and peaceful countrysides covered with the innocence of wildflowers and bird songs. That a certain beauty exists in Appalachia cannot be denied. The Trans-America guidebook states:

> The word Appalachia brings to mind thoughts of simple frame houses, moonshine and stills, banjos and porch swings, and tiny farms nestled in the bottoms of the "hollers." It is all these things and more.

It is also a canopy of dense foliage; of oak, hickory and maple; steep and narrow valleys; and 100 different streams and swimming holes.

It is not an easy section to cross; rather it is probably the most demanding 200-plus miles of all. In Appalachia your cycling consists of only two things: grinding up steep hills and then coasting down. The road builders did not believe in switchbacks.

The Trans-America guidebook warns the cyclist: "About 20 miles east of Berea the real challenge begins. Gravel roads, broken pavement, and low-water bridges are all a part of the route through the back country of Appalachia."

Traffic is generally low in this country except for the coal trucks. Most of the roads are narrow and two laners with no shoulders. Overloaded coal trucks are hauling the entire state of Kentucky away while the naive natives stand on sagging front porches and wave at the passing remains. Seven or eight companies from outside Kentucky own 94 percent of the mineral rights. Meanwhile, 25 percent of the people living in the state are on welfare. Tens of millions of dollars of coal left the state at the time when a country school teacher earned a mere $75 per month.

Carrying 30 tons of coal, these trucks would come screaming down the steep grades and around the curves at the maximum speed limit, their tires pulverizing the road into wide cracks and chuck holes. Huge chunks of coal would fly off, and the roadway and shoulders were littered with 20-pound coal rocks. Cars would not follow too closely behind because many a car driver reported a smashed hood caused by the flying coal. Just imagine the poor biker. According to my journal, ''Whenever we heard one of these behemoths behind we would try our best to get out of their way. By the end of the day we were covered and grimy with the coal dust that floated in the air.''

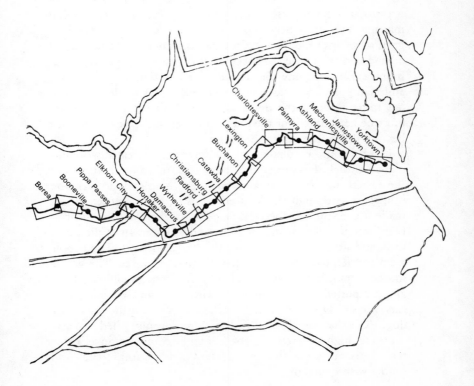

The whole thing was depressing.

Marshall Strickler felt no love for this part of the country:

After Berea, the road deteriorated into three to four miles of gravel, then a very poor surface, and Kentucky did an abrupt about face! It was as though she got caught in the rain. The mascara ran, the lipstick smeared, the color washed out of her hair, and all of a sudden there was Kentucky. A blowsy, down-at-the-heels slattern, smoking a corncob pipe and siccing the hounds on "them flat-land bicyclers!" It is really hard to understand how one state could change so drastically, and so rapidly — ravishing rural beauty one day and disreputable "junque" the very next moment.

We are into coal mining country with a vengeance, so the roads are extremely hazardous. The roads wind up and down between the knobs, following stream beds as best they can. The coal trucks roar up and down these roads as close to wide open as they can manage. They carry heavy loads and, as a result, have chewed up great sections of the road. More often than not you come around a bend and the entire cross-section of the road has disintegrated. If you are making any speed at all, there is a grasping of brakes and manipulation of steering as you seek to pick the least hazardous route through the devastation. And all the time, one ear must be kept tuned for the oncoming roar of the next coal truck bearing down from either direction.

I wish I could emphasize adequately what a great disappointment Kentucky has turned out to be. It is truly a lovely state, but the eastern half has been allowed to go completely to rack and ruin. It is as though the least enterprising of the settlers barely made it over the Cumberland Gap, broke their wagons, pushed them into the nearest stream beds, and squatted amid their own trash and litter, not to move for the next 200 years. The people seem unfriendly. There were few welcoming waves. The gentle southern tradition of saying "Hey" is foregone. Members of our group reported being bombarded with beer cans, banana peels, ears of corn. Others reported overhearing one worthy say to her dog, "Git that bicyclist!" Roadsides are slovenly, piled two and three feet high with trash, garbage, and litter of every imaginable type. Junk cars are everywhere. Stream beds are full of trash and murky with debris of every sort.

Dave Brown remembers:

Riding in Kentucky was like sailing on a cornfield sea amid green hills. Almost every morning we rode in ground fog which took all morning for the sun to burn away. It seemed like the trees didn't want to release their grasp on the gray veil. It gave us a spooky feeling of disorder as we rode up and down the hills which we could not really see, over a road which was not defined except for the space just ahead of us. My glasses often became fogged, and I could not see where I was going. My friend, who had bright yellow panniers, rode directly ahead of me, and I visually hung onto those panniers for dear life lest he pull away from me. Even so, I still ran downhill many a time in this fog more by feel than by sight.

As we neared the Appalachians we began to hear more and more "horror" stories about these hills from the people who were heading west. We found out for ourselves that they were not as scary as we had been told. The roads were very narrow and more closed in with trees so you could not see as far as you could in the Rockies and even the Ozarks. Sometimes the road would be a tunnel of overlapping tree branches. We figured that they were challenging to the westbound riders because they met them in their second week of riding while we had all summer to get into condition.

However, the stories we had heard about the people were true. They were often outright hostile. There were very few friendly encounters and none that I experienced on a one-to-one basis. We would be camping in the city parks and invariably the locals would show their disrespect for the campers by taking great delight in roaring their junk cars through our area very late at night. They can also keep their bugs. The jiggers and ticks were unreal.

The happy respite to our Appalachian travels came in Pippa Passes, where not only were we treated to the delicious home-cooked food of the Maddens, but to a Shakespeare festival at Alice Lloyd College. You have not experienced Shakespeare until you have heard it in a southern accent.

As far as enjoying the general scenery, I was able to look beyond the trash heaps; not that they did not still exist, but I could see the beauty that was there — the unplanned architecture of the barns and farms as if they were scattered helter-skelter from some unseen hand, the smallness of the farms, and the simplicity of that lifestyle.

It is interesting to note that the two most memorable bike inns were both located in this state. Falls of Rough, the least popular, was located in the pretty western half of Kentucky, while this miserable eastern half supported Pippa Passes. The bike innkeepers, Mr. and Mrs. Madden, day after day all summer long provided every biker with a home cooked meal worth writing home about. This was a most welcome change from the blank unfriendly stares of the locals. Also in Pippa Passes is found the small junior college, Alice Lloyd, with its neat well-tended grounds instead of the poverty-ridden shacks and weed patches.

Food continues to be readily accessible because of the closeness of each town. Lodging, however, in eastern Kentucky is another thing. The towns are too small or too poor to support any type of hotel or motel, but camping areas are easily obtained.

Near the stateline of Virginia, Kentucky shows a cleaner face almost by way of apology. Often called the "Grand Canyon of the South with Clothes On," the deep river gorge of the Breaks Interstate Park plunges down between tree-covered mountains for almost 3,000 feet. From here you have a chance to view the area for the last time — much to almost everyone's great relief.

Is it true what they say about Appalachia? Well, I guess you will just have to find out for yourself.

Verdant Virginia

Virginia is everything that Kentucky could have been. It rivals anything you could see in the Rockies and then some. In a quiet way all its own, it is the loveliest state of all. The terrain changes almost immediately upon crossing the stateline; like the morning mist, the roadside trash vanishes, and is replaced by wild blackberry vines creeping over fence posts and dew-sprinkled spider webs covering the lush blades of grass.

The choppy hills of Appalachia become long ridges of the Allegheny and Blue Ridge Mountains with only a few very steep sections. The open land is rolling farmland once again, and friendliness is seen on the faces of the Virginians.

The heat and humidity are also a part of this country, and the heavy air smells of ripening huckleberries, new mown hay, and damp grass. The roads are narrow, but lightly traveled with swooping curves and gentle grades. Our biking trail was one of crossing streams and following rivers.

The valley of Virginia, or the Great Valley, separates the younger and older Appalachian Mountains. It is actually a series of valleys divided by small knolls and ridges. The largest basin in the Great Valley is that of the Shenandoah Valley. Words fall far short of being able to describe that valley. Smoky blue-forested ridges shrouded with mist repeat and repeat into infinity. Soft green meadows spread like an endless carpet at your feet with no billboards or litter to spoil the "augenblinks." The pastoral charm and simplicity of the farms make you feel that perhaps the whole world has become a peaceful place.

By all means, elect to ride part of the Blue Ridge Parkway even though there is the alternate valley floor route. Your efforts in climbing Vesuvius Hill to the top are well rewarded. (Vesuvius Hill is supposed to be the most challenging, steepest hill on the entire trail.) You certainly can choose any number of other, less challenging routes to the Blue Ridge. One would be to follow Route 60 eastward out of Lexington. Although there are not any campgrounds on the Blue Ridge Parkway, there are many places to choose from elsewhere along the route, and food stores and full service towns are all within easy riding distance.

The Trans-America Trail uses only a 30-mile section of the Blue Ridge Parkway although it is 575 miles in total length. Running between the two states of Virginia and North Carolina, it was originally conceived in 1909, but it took about 30 years for the project to be completed. The Appalachian Trail, a hiking trail which runs from Maine to Georgia, parallels or crosses the Blue Ridge Parkway several times. Most of the valley floor is at elevations of 1,000 feet and less, while the Parkway dips and soars along at 3,000 feet. Enjoy the bird's eye view.

When I was in the early stages of packing for my cross-country trip, I wanted to select a book which I knew would fill the quiet times with hours of enjoyable reading. Having decided that one reading was not enough of *Pilgrim at Tinker Creek* by Annie Dillard, I chose it as the one book I wanted to have with me. In a way, I felt like a pilgrim in this undertaking — one who would rediscover my country. But like Annie, I hoped to find the tiny things that give meaning to life and the world around us hidden beneath the large surface of things. Little did I know that the Trans-America Trail would go right next to and around Tinker Mountain. Unlike other bikers not acquainted with Tinker Mountain and much less intimate with it, I saw it as a very special place. I vicariously traveled to Tinker Creek with Annie and found a very special place teeming with life and adventure.

Every biker dreams of someday finding the "perfect road." Well, I am one of the lucky ones; I found it! One of the most delightful roads for cycling is Route 723 between Christiansburg and Daleville, Virginia. This perfect road follows the Roanoke Valley for miles and miles, tracing every bend of the Roanoke River. The road hangs suspended on the side of a ridge about 150 feet above the valley floor. Across the valley the green, hazy Blue Ridge hills parallel the scene. The July morning of my ride was also a perfect day. I had a tail wind, a blue sky, and a summer Saturday to spend in the Virginia countryside. The road was blacktopped and smooth. There were no towns for 45 miles, and no traffic. The valley was mine, the morning was mine, and it was a beautiful day. Farms followed farms throughout the country, one weathered barn leading to the next — all with immaculate, neat barnyards — on and on. And all the while, the hazy, silent hills contained the day.

Fun uphills and fast downhills — rolling and curving with the swinging, shining river below — toward Tinker Mountain with its wild flowers. The country was mine. I felt as if I owned the world and was sitting on top of it all. The birds and the butterflies danced through the weeds, and the trees were mine. With wide-eyed abandon and wonderment, I traveled through the day. If the summer were to have ended with this day, the journey could not have been more complete. The long summer had reached its climax. It was now rushing to its finish, and soon this odyssey would be tied in a bundle with memory's string and carried under my arm back home.

Across the long valley, the Blue Ridge Mountains held my vision — my very being — this day. How can anything east of the Rockies be as beautiful as this?

It seems that there is more history in Virginia than in any other Bikecentennial state, but maybe more of it has simply been preserved here. You come close to Thomas Jefferson, Stonewall Jackson, and Robert E. Lee. You find Lexington and Charlottesville and Williamsburg — towns where history is alive and well. Here is Washington and Lee University with the famous Lee Chapel; one floor has been made into a museum containing many of the general's personal belongings. Virginia Military Institute is here with its gothic architecture and General George C. Marshall Memorial Library, named for a famous graduate. Monticello was Thomas Jefferson's home, and the University of Virginia was designed by Jefferson. There is the completely restored colonial town of Williamsburg. All of these places are not to be missed. In Jamestown and Yorktown are found the "roots" of this country — its very beginnings.

Near Richmond are many Civil War battle sites. Since Richmond was the capital of the Confederacy, Virginia was a major battleground. Between Ashton and Charles City, the Trans-America Trail "walks" in the footsteps of those who engaged in the "Battle of Seven Days." Several cemeteries line the road, as well as the remains of the trenches and other earthworks.

Lexington, a very historical city with excellent examples of architecture from the colonial and Civil War eras, offers a walking tour where 100 years of history intertwine with present-day living.

By the time you reach the Piedmont and Tidewater regions, the elevation is only 200 feet above sea level, a gently rolling plain slanting toward the Atlantic Ocean. The only thing that is rising is the humidity. The land has flattened out into the broad coastal plain and finally becomes very level along the James River. Also known as Plantation Row, many of the opulent estates still stand in perfect repair. These are the homes of the favored ones of King James of England, who were rewarded with hundreds and thousands of acres of New World land upon which to build red brick and white frame pillared mansions. From those earliest times, great fields of tobacco were the major source of income and the owners of the huge plantations depended upon slaves, as well as tobacco, to maintain their luxurious lifestyles. Small, self-sustaining farms grow corn, hay, wheat, and oats, as well as tobacco.

My journal records:

> Around the time of the Civil War, a man named Kent began a general store on a crossroads corner in Virginia. It is still called Kent's Store today. On a very, very hot and humid afternoon more than 100 years later, I stopped at Kent's Store. The original building had long since burned down, and another store was erected directly across the way almost 50 years ago. The "new" store is a long, brown, wooden structure with a full-length porch and bench facing the world for sitting and watching and looking and talking. A planter full of geraniums is at each end. From this porch a rolling pasture, corn field, and the woods beyond can be seen. A couple of weathered barns squat at the edge of the pasture. And that today is the town of Kent's Store — almost like it always was.
>
> How delightful it is to find places that do not change with time. I almost expected to find old man Kent behind the counter. It was somewhat cooler inside. "Well, here comes someone who looks hot. They have been rinsing off back there." I followed the direction of the pointing arm of the lady behind the cash drawer. I really did look hot. As soon as you stop the air flow, the sweat begins to just pour off. A bottle of orange soda later, I was down to normal. We made the usual small talk. "Where ya goin'? Where ya from? You mean ya started way from there? My, that's a long way! How far did ya all ride today?"
>
> "Not very far. I spent most of the day at Michie's Tavern, Monticello, and Ash Lawn. I am also thinking about camping anytime now in the woods."
>
> "You can stay here if ya like. Some bikers have put up their tents in the backyard; or you can sleep in the store if ya like to."

And that is how I happened to spend the remainder of the day at Kent's Store. After Tots, the owner of Kent's Store, closed for the day, we retired to her rear apartment and shared conversation and beer until the small hours of the morning.

The End Is Near

There were hundreds of country stores, each with its own personal style of friendliness and always the same questions. About the only thing that changed were the accents as you moved across the country. There is something earthy about a country store. I was happy to learn that the store with the potbelly stove is alive and well and thriving in all the small towns and on all the "Main Streets" of America. Almost always they are run by outgoing, uncomplicated people.

As the final miles were rolling away into another place in time, a different sense of urgency was forming. There is a rush of body and mind toward Yorktown. All the mountains are behind, the anticipation of late May becoming the calm satisfaction of late August. The land, as well as your driving pedals, propel you onward. The days tend to mesh into one long continuous time, and the last few remaining miles are a real cakewalk. The end of the trip is counted in hours instead of miles or even days. Along with the urgent eagerness to reach Yorktown, that place of our journey's end, there was also the nagging knowledge that the end of the adventure of a lifetime was almost over. There begins the feeling that maybe by looking longer or by taking more time to get down the road — almost like shifting into slow motion — that the ending could be delayed a little longer.

Anticipation rewarded with fulfillment surged through the bodies of over 2,000 cyclists as each reached the shores of their destinations. So many times the anticipation is always greater than the reward, and that has always been an accepted fact of life. At least the desire brought some enjoyment. Never mind that it is almost always reversed. For each of the 2,000 cyclists, however, I am almost sure that the summer of 1976 was most rewarding.

An interesting side note to this narration is the observation that someone riding east to west would naturally have a totally different set of perspectives. Going westward, a fairly large number of riders were also anxious to reach Reedsport, Oregon.

By mid-July many riders were meeting and passing each other along the trail. Each side had their stories to tell — an exchange of times past for those of times future. Each was interested in the other's impressions because that is where they would be shortly. So each listened well and at last wished each other "Godspeed."

And to all of you who dream of this trip, today vicariously, tomorrow for real, I wish you a most happy journey.

part 3

Maintenance and Miscellaneous Thoughts

13

Keeping Your Bike Happy

Do not begin any tour, even a weekender, on a "tired" bicycle. Sooner or later, something is going to snap due to lack of attention on your part. I am sure you know of bikers who do nothing to their bicycles. They look pretty grungy, but these bikers ride and ride, and nothing ever happens to them. Well, someday....

Everyone should learn to tinker with their bicycles. One easy way to get into that habit is to start with a bicycle you really like. Interestingly enough, if you hate even the color of your present bike, you won't like it at all. Short of buying a new one, you could repaint it, but if you are still in the buying market, do get one you like.

There are several ways you can learn about the heart and soul of your pride. There are two good books you can read for starters: *Glenn's Complete Bicycle Manual* by Clarence Coles and Harold Glenn and Fred DeLong's book, *DeLong's Guide to Bicycles and Bicycling*. Glenn's manual has easy-to-follow, step-by-step photo illustrations leading you through all aspects of the bicycle. If your friendly bike shop is really friendly, the mechanic may be willing to take some time to explain things to you, or you may know of some knowledgeable riders who will take you under their wings.

At least try to overhaul it yourself. Short of buggering up the bottom bracket threads, there is little you can do that cannot be easily corrected, and at the same dollar cost to you as if you had simply taken the bike in for an overhaul in the first place.

Doing all your own repairs will, of course, teach you what makes your bicycle tick. There is no more mystery, and you can travel the road with confidence. Who cares if you are 200 miles in the middle of nowhere? After all, the idea is to be totally self-contained and self-sufficient, isn't it? Somehow, having to hitch a ride takes something away from being able to say "I rode the entire distance."

The purpose of this chapter is not to tell you how to overhaul a bicycle. The two suggested books can do that. Besides, you should not overhaul a bicycle on the road, but at home. However, there are a number of parts which do require regular maintenance and a few parts which require daily checking. There are only two types of repairs that you should ever have to make on the road — that's right, only two. And they can even be narrowed down to only one, the good old flat tire. If your wheels are in good shape, you should be able to travel 5,000 — 10,000 miles before breaking a spoke. But, like flat tires, spokes choose to snap at the worst possible times for any number of reasons.

Flat Tires

Just like I would not take the car anywhere without its spare tire, I do not go anywhere by bicycle without the wherewithal to fix flats. I always carry an extra inner tube because, rather than patch the tire along the side of the road, it is easier to patch the hole in a comfortable area — especially one with access to water since many holes are too small to find unless the tube can be blown up and dunked.

Before you remove the rear wheel, if that is the flat, make sure that the chain is on the smallest freewheel cog. This makes it so much easier to drop the wheel. If you push forward on the wheel at the same time you pull the derailleur back and out of the way, the wheel should roll right off.

1.   Now that we have removed the wheel, take one of your tire irons, not a screwdriver or a knife blade or any other pointed object, but a genuine bicycle tire iron and starting opposite the valve stem, insert the iron under the lip or bead of the tire. All the steps in tire repair either begin or end opposite the valve (see Figure 13.1).

FIGURE 13.1

Valve
Stem

2.   Hook the other end around the nearest and most convenient spoke and leave it in that position (see Figure 13.2).
3.   Taking your second tire iron, hook it under the lip near to
the first iron and gently and carefully lever the tire over the rim,
moving a couple of inches or so around the circumference of the
rim. Relax enough tension so that you can then slide the second
tire iron around the bead until the entire side is over the rim.

FIGURE 13.2

Note the first tire iron is still in place for the entire step (see Figure 13.3).

4.   Reach under the bead and grab the inner tube, then pull it out completely. (Unless you know exactly where the puncture is and intend to patch it right then and there, you can leave the rest of the inner tube on the rim.) As you pull out the inner tube, you will want to work toward the valve. Bend the tire back and away from over the valve stem, and remove the inner tube completely off the rim. Now check for the cause of your problem. At least take the end of the tire iron and run it all around

FIGURE 13.3

First Tire Iron Still in Place

the inside of the tire. But be careful. If you do not get it, you could very well end up with another hole (see Figure 13.4).

5.   Your choice now is either to patch the tire or put in your replacement tube. If you patch the tire, be sure that the surface is dry and properly roughed with coarse sandpaper or the little metal scratcher. After you are certain that the glue is completely and absolutely dry, apply the patch and burnish the edges with the tire iron for a good seal.

6.   With the new or repaired inner tube insert the valve stem first. Make sure that it is perpendicular to the rim and not canted over at a 45 degree angle. That action will cause the rim holes to cut the valve stem. Working from the valve stem, stuff the inner tube back inside the tire, and place the tire under the lip of the rim. Continue working away from the valve, one hand on either side of the rim. Use your thumb to work the tire back

FIGURE 13.4

Valve
Stem

on the rim, stuffing the inner tube in as you go (see Figure 13.5).

7.   Continue doing this until both hands come together at the opposite edge from the valve stem. By now you should have all but seven inches or so of tire still hanging over the rim. Unless you have a very new, unstretched, stubborn tire, you should never, never have to use the tire iron to snap the remaining tire over the rim. Use your thumbs or the heel of your hand to snap it over the rim, making sure the inner tube is all the way in. Sometimes, but not often, it takes strong thumbs to get the snap, but with an older tire it can be done quite easily. Using a tire iron quite often will result in making another puncture. I know; I have done it. Check all around the rim to see that the tube is well within the tire and not hanging outside the bead, and then inflate the tire. With practice, this minor repair is nothing more than a ten-minute delay (see Figure 13.6).

FIGURE 13.5

FIGURE 13.6

Broken Spokes

Replacing a spoke is easy if you have the one all-important tool — the freewheel remover. Spokes almost always break on the freewheel side of the rear wheel, so we will detail that problem. The same procedure can be followed from the third step onward for broken spokes elsewhere.

There are some really strange freewheels which either were never meant to be removed even with their specific remover, or almost require the hub to be disassembled in order to get the re-mover seated on the freewheel. Probably the two easiest free-wheels to remove are the Suntour or Shimano. They are also the two most common freewheels today. Sometimes it is easier with the few off-beat, difficult ones to actually take the freewheel cogs off and get down to the hub flange. Use either the chain-like freewheel tool or, if you are on the road, your own bicycle chain. If you have to go to those extremes to do a simple spoke replacement, you would be further ahead to spend the few dollars for one of the above recommended freewheels.

The principle with freewheel removal, for those of you who have never seen a naked rear hub, is this: as a unit it is screwed onto the hub just like a nut onto a bolt. In essence, all you are doing is unscrewing a nut — in this case, the freewheel. It is not going to fall apart in a million pieces when you put a wrench to it.

1.   When you do not have a vise handy, it is always a good idea to use the hub skewer to hold the freewheel remover in place (see Figure 13.7)

2.   With at least a nine-inch crescent wrench and the axle skewer in place, turn counterclockwise. Be careful that the skewer is tight enough so that the remover will not slip off and chew up the grooves. It should be loose enough to allow room for the unscrewing. It should take a one-half turn to break the freewheel loose. Hold the tire with your left hand and bear down on the wrench with your right hand. Notice that the wrench is to the left as you face the wheel. That one-half turn should be enough to enable you to unscrew the freewheel the rest of the way by turning the remover by hand. Remove the skewer first since it was needed only to hold the remover steady (see Figure 13.8).

FIGURE 13.7

Axle Skewer

Freewheel
Remover
Tool

Direction of Turn or Leverage

Axle Skewer Nut Holding Freewheel Remover Tool in Place

FIGURE 13.8

3. You can now observe the spokes. They alternate head in or head out around the hub flange. Be sure that you install the replacement spoke exactly like the broken one (see Figure 13.9).
4. Pull it all the way through the hole making sure that it is seated properly. Bring it up toward the rim. Now you will have to deflate your tire to get under the rim strip and the inner tube to remove what remains of the broken spoke. Drop the new spoke nipple into the same hole. The spoke nipple is that screwlike piece that the spoke threads into. Also notice how the neighboring spokes were crossed and make sure that you cross your spoke exactly the same way. When you are sure it is exactly right, fit the threaded end into the nipple and give the nipple a few turns with your fingers (see Figure 13.10).
5. Take your spoke wrench and tighten it from here. When the spoke broke, tension was released at that point, and the wheel was pulled out of alignment over to the other side. You probably noticed that the wheel was rubbing against the brake pad

FIGURE 13.9

FIGURE 13.10

and so on. What you want to do is pull the wheel back to where it belongs by tightening the new spoke just the proper amount. You may have to loosen or tighten the adjoining spokes to get it exactly right, but easy does it. With the wheel back on the bike, use the brake pads as alignment guides. Work in terms of one-quarter turns at a time. With practice, wheel trueing comes easier. If in doubt, you can always have a bike shop check the wheel on their trueing stand.

6.   I always leave replacing the freewheel to the very last, because sometimes in retrueing the wheel another spoke could break, and then you have to unscrew it again. When screwing the freewheel back on be careful that you do not cross-thread or strip the threads. It goes on very easily if you get the threads properly lined up. Use your hands for this step; it is okay as long as it is finger tight. The first pedal revolution will tighten it completely.

Daily Checklist

If you are in the habit of tinkering already, the following counsel will be automatic for you. Every morning there are six things you should check without fail. These include the following:

The Tires.   Pinch them to check for proper air pressure. They usually lose a few pounds every day or two. Look at the tread and make sure that nothing has cut either it or the side wall.

Wheel Alignment.   How many bumps and potholes did you find yesterday? Spin both wheels and using either a brake pad or a frame stay, make sure that your wheels are true and not wiggling from side to side or hopping with flat spots.

The Brakes.   They should work fast, smoothly, and not bind up. Cables do stretch, especially when they are new, so make sure that you still have at least one and a half inches between the levers and the handlebars when the pads are tight against the rims. Make sure that the pads are not worn and also that they align with the rims. They should not be rubbing against any part of the tire.

The Chain.   On a long tour the chain needs oil every second or third day. WD-40 or LPS-3 works fine. Always carry a small can with you. You can make a neat job of oiling your chain if you hold a rag, or better still a paper towel, behind the chain somewhere between the rear derailleur and chain crank. Give a squirt to the chain, catching any overspray on the towel. Then, using the towel which is in your cupped right hand, pull the chain toward the crank (as if you were backpedaling) and repeat until the entire length has a new coating of oil.

The Cables.   They last a long time, but any kinks in the housing will cause them to bind up. There is a new brake housing on the market called Elephant Cable which has a teflon inner lining and is *smoooooth*. It is well worth your trouble to install it.

The Headset.   Grab the drops of the handlebars as you do in a riding position and hold on the front brake. Then rock the bike forward and backward. If there is any play or "slapping," then your headset needs to be tightened. It requires a ten-inch crescent wrench, something which is not usually carried in the biker's tool kit, but one that you should find easily enough at almost any gas station or garage. Tighten the top ring about one-half turn short of tight. (How tight is tight? If in doubt, have a bike shop show you.) Then tighten the lock nut down on it.

Then for good measure, check all screws and bolts. They sometimes do manage to vibrate loose.

A bicycle is a very uncomplicated piece of equipment. Everything about it is visible and easy to get to. Another way of rationalizing do-it-yourself bike repair is to consider that for the cost of an overhaul you can just about purchase the necessary tools!

14

1976 — That Was the Year That Was

All of the 4,065 men and women from the U.S. and 16 other countries who rode all or part of the Trans-America Trail saw an America that is not often seen from the fast-paced super highway. For many like Marshall Strickler:

> It was the single, most memorable and meaningful experience in my life. Each day we found ourselves growing stronger. Long distances and high passes no longer boggled our minds. Riding had become second nature. Instead, you spent time enjoying the beautiful changing scenery of rural America, still much as it was when our forefathers made the long trek on foot, horseback or in wagon.

His last journal entry went like this:

> It's hard to believe this trip, an all-American blockbuster, is over. My total mileage is 4,274 miles, but the country seems

smaller after covering it foot-by-foot. The daily news and conventions of living have taken on new perspectives, too. I've got a greater appreciation and understanding of America's impressiveness than ever before — its beauty and strength.

For many persons, the riding of this bicycle trail was their first experience with long distance bicycle travel. Approximately 36 percent of the riders reported their total touring mileage was below 400 miles prior to their Bikecentennial tour. The Bikecentennial program did much to encourage all cyclists to participate, regardless of previous experience, by placing emphasis on the group tours. This approach was meant to encourage riders with limited experience to gain the confidence and cycling ability so that they would want to tour independently in the future. As part of a group, they would have a trained leader, maps and guidebooks, group equipment like tools, cooking supplies, first aid kits, and a health/accident insurance policy. Several publications designed to help in getting them ready for the tour were mailed to each participant prior to departure. All these procedures are still employed since Bikecentennial is now an ongoing thing.

One of the Trans-America leaders, Lloyd Sumner, had this to say about his group and the trip in general:

> Next morning we cycled the empty Duke of Gloucester Street in Williamsburg before rolling on down the Colonial Parkway to Yorktown. Suddenly, just ahead to the left was the Victory monument, the official end of the Trans-America Trail. The happiness of completing a major endeavor was mingled with the sadness of breaking up the group. But before there were any tears either way, someone was heard to shout, "Well, here we are."
>
> As I think back on the Bikecentennial summer, several special memories keep recurring: cycling in the invigorating predawn air, waving to farmers in their fields, laughing with the birds that flew along in companionship, pumping level miles beneath our feet across the infinite expanses of Kansas, and watching a collection of 12 individuals mold themselves into a spirited unit.
>
> But the real thrill of these memories is that they were echoed

all across the country by thousands of other riders and will be enjoyed by thousands more in the years to come. Bikecentennial is a great beginning.

In the year or two before the summer of '76, the field teams began to make arrangements for lodging and bike inns in all the small towns. They were met with reserve and apprehension. "You mean thousands of bikers are coming through our quiet town?" Words such as strangers, hippy, footloose were common. There was doubt and a certain amount of ambivalence, too. The people back at Bikecentennial headquarters quickly began to realize where their endeavors might lead. "If Bikecentennial fails, it will surely drag all of bicycling down with it."

All during the bicentennial summer, with the thousands of cyclists now arriving in the towns, Bikecentennial could only wait to see what would happen. They had made it a point time and again, at the leadership training courses that each leader was responsible for every rider in his or her group and that any unacceptable social or moral action should not be tolerated. By their very nature and habits, the cyclists did establish an image of safe, courteous bicycle travelers. An overwhelming 97 percent of the cyclists said they had found the people in the communities friendly and receptive toward them. Informal interviewing of the people in the communities revealed a similar enthusiastic response toward the cyclists.

As the cyclists became daily visitors, the people along the trail began to get into the spirit of the adventure. The bikers were accepted warmly and gladly. Such things as crude hand-letterd signs began to appear in front of farm houses, restaurants, and grocery stores. "Bikers welcome, free drinks and ice water." One grocery store in a small town in Kansas displayed a huge sign in its window, "Welcome Bikers!! Come in — use our air conditioned lounge. Free coffee, ice water, rest rooms."

Another thing that was quite common all across the land was the "guest book" that accompanied these invitations. "Would you sign your name for us?" was asked many times over. The book varied from the leather-bound edition to a well-worn loose-leaf notebook. There was space for the date, name, address, and how far you were riding. This ritual, of course, opened up untold avenues of conversation. It seemed the people never tired of the associations. For the bikers, they reveled in the notoriety. But the books also became a way of finding out whether a friend was ahead, and if so, how far. Comments were added, and eventually messages were left recorded between the pages for a friend a day or so behind. Like links in a chain, this "family" of Bikecentennial cyclists knew or could find the whereabouts of every one of its members, even though they were spread across the breadth and width of the land.

Thousands of words have been written about one family in particular, and every cyclist who kept a journal that summer surely recorded something about the Norman Parker family of Hebron, Colorado.

Hebron is a place in the middle of a vast landscape between Walden and Kremmling. There are no other towns. A railroad crossing and a sign are all there is to tell you you have arrived in Hebron. The total town stands alongside the tracks and consists of a single, white frame house and a few outbuildings. By the side of the road stands another crudely lettered sign to welcome bikers to stop for refreshments. There were lemonade and home baked cookies sitting on top of an old school desk. According to the two redheaded lads who appeared, we had to sign our names in the inevitable notebook before partaking of the goodies. Taking no donations, the Parkers paid for the thousands of cookies out of their own pocket, but they felt they were well rewarded by the hundreds of experiences they had during the summer.

Another smaller sign said "Come up to the house and say hello if you have the time." We went inside because time was forgotten — lost somewhere to another lifestyle. There was a 12-string guitar standing in a living room corner. As expected, someone could play it, and the song — "What a Day for a Daydream" — summarized the mood and setting. A gesture was returned for the hospitality and warmth found so unexpectedly.

Terry and Betty Noble of Corvallis, Montana, also claim that the Bikecentennial was the highlight of their summer. Every afternoon bikers from all over the world were under their big maple tree. They said: "And what a delight these people were. There were students, teachers, doctors, a carpenter from Sweden, a musician from Mexico City, bike teams from Holland, and families."

Then there was June Curry, "The Cookie Lady" of Ashton, Virginia. Her friendly, red brick house sits tight against the road at the top of a very steep and winding road leading down to the Coastal Plain. Early in the summer, she began to notice an unusual number of cyclists passing her house regularly. A cyclist one day told her that he was riding to Oregon, that many more would be following, and that by late July hundreds would be coming from the opposite direction, having started several months before in Oregon.

Although she never had learned to ride a bicycle herself, she admired the adventurous spirits of "these brightly dressed and happy people." From that day on, snacks, fruit, cold drinks, and sandwiches were spread out on a table on her front porch. In no time via the Biker's grapevine, her house in Ashton was a "you-must-stop-there" place high on every cyclist's list.

According to a Bikecentennial survey sent to all participants, the report showed that all the cyclists who took part in the adventure were middle-class urbanites, and most were well educated, with 78 percent having some college or college degrees. Only 4 percent considered themselves unemployed. As a group, their lifestyles and habits reflected a concern with ecology, safety, health, and nutrition.

Bikecentennial was basically adult oriented, and the majority of riders was between the ages of 17 and 35. The ages ranged, however, from 7 to 86 years. The oldest known rider to complete the entire trail was 67, while two 9-year-olds were the youngest.

Everyone remembers Clarence Pickard, the 86-year-old Iowa farmer who rode from Yorktown into Missouri — about 1,500 miles before quitting. He said so many people — reporters and town folk alike — wanted to talk to him; as a result it took him all day to complete the distance and rejoin his group.

Bikecentennial meant, for some, an unusual vacation. But for

others it was a personal challenge. It afforded many an opportunity to grow emotionally as well as physically. Crossing this
continent under the power of one's own body instills a great
feeling of confidence that anything can be accomplished. The
rewards are an individual matter, and each person cherishes the
summer's memories.

Jay Anderson, another trip leader, remembers:

> It took 81 days to cover about 4,200 miles. We suffered 19 days
> of precipitation, including two days of snow in the northern Rock-
> ies, and on our final day, we arrived in Williamsburg, Virginia,
> along with Hurricane Belle. Our worse accident was bike-on-bike.
> Our worst repair job was a broken axle. Thirteen of us were hit by
> a 24-hour virus in Kentucky.
>
> For myself, I had eight flat tires, eight broken spokes, and a
> broken chain. I went through three sets of tires and two pairs of
> cycling gloves. I suffered only a mild cold in Colorado and had
> no serious spills. I lost about ten pounds and two waistline inches.
>
> Did I enjoy it? Would I do it again? Of course! Rather than
> take away the wanderlust, the trip only whetted my appetite. Do
> you ask why? Let me tell you about this seven-mile downhill just
> out of Virginia City into Ennis....

Appendix 1

Alpha and Omega
of a Journey*

Someone said "How would you like to ride a bicycle 4,300 miles all across America, from coast to coast?" At first it sounded crazy, then intriguing, fantastic, impossible. Why not? It would be a fun trip. Could I do it?

The idea had been conceived and it was growing. Like mushrooms. The more I thought about it, the more I wanted to do it. Until one day I said somewhat nonchalantly, "I am going to bicycle across America!" It was settled at last. The road out was straight, broad, and ever sun-dappled. The journey was clearly defined and contained within two oceans on something called the Trans-America Trail.

Now all I had to do was pack the panniers and get to the coast. For days I made lists, added things, took away, remade the lists, wrestled with the growing weight. Too much. But I

*This article was published in the *Arizona Bicycle Club Newsletter*.

need this; I simply want that. I was so taken with the problems of preparation, the great venture of daring took second place.

Not until I was at the airport with the cumbersome box marked "Bicycle," did I become aware of what I was going to do. "I am going to ride, no, pedal across America! I must be crazy." But the sense of adventure continued to beckon with a persistent finger. I was eager to get started, but just below the surface lurked a tear or two born of apprehension. Three months away from family, friends, and those familiar surroundings.

That tight feeling sat in my throat all during the flight. I had been on one other bicycle tour and that was only a 400-miler. I was wound up like a spring. I kept going over in my mind the enticing photos of the Oregon coast. How beautiful a place. I told myself, I shall see that beautiful place, I shall touch the wind and the rocks along the coast and share my freedom with the sea gulls.

But it wasn't like that at all when at last I found myself standing on a sand promontory looking out to sea. The wind was cold this second day of May and the sky was heavy with rain clouds. I was all alone and apprehension had once again clouded my beautiful mental pictures. It began to drizzle. I started to feel miserable, to question my sanity. Suddenly, the United States became gigantic beyond belief and impossible ever to cross on a bicycle. The bike moved like it was made out of lead; my legs felt like wood. I fiddled with the gears so carefully planned and nothing seemed right. "This is a flat road, why am I in such a low gear?" I fidgeted with the clothes and was convinced that everything I brought along was wrong. I worried the entire afternoon away instead of touching the sea air and sharing my freedom. What freedom! I was beginning to feel very lonely. I knew for certain now I really was crazy. Yet, I kept telling myself there are few things I would rather do than travel and ride my bicycle, and here I have an entire summer to do both. Common sense finally took over and at Cape Lookout State Park I decided to camp for the night.

The making of camp was done by rote. The familiar tasks were habits established from a countless number of backpacking trips. As soon as the tent and sleeping bag were in place, the

sense of adventure came flooding back. Late that evening a soli-
tary walk along the beach restored my feeling of self-confidence.
Just take one day at a time and let the adventure happen at its
own pace; never mind contemplating the finish. Such a simple
revelation. I was excited once again over the thought that the
entire summer was ahead of me. Instead of recalling to mind
that monster map of the United States, I pulled from my pocket
a small folded piece of a map showing the Oregon coast, and I
became engrossed in the names as my finger followed the red
line of my route. Tillamook. Haystack Rock. Netarts Bay. Cape
Meares.

Tomorrow. And all the tomorrows of summer I shall come to
know these places and a million more by sight as well as name.
Maps are such enchanting things. Mine, that small scrap of paper, had erased the last vestige of doubt and the remainder of
the evening was spent touching the air and the rocks and sharing
my renewed sense of exhilarated freedom with the waves and
the sea gulls.

So the summer passed, and each day held its own adventure
as was promised so long ago on that cold and windy evening on
the Oregon coast. I spent a week there exploring bays and capes
and small towns while at the same time taking part in and passing the leadership training school of the Bikecentennial '76
Tour. My total trip was divided between leading several short
tours and riding independently. Now, three months later, it was
all finished. Done. With tires screaming of 5,000 miles, I roared
into downtown Yorktown, Virginia.

And I stopped.

And I looked about me. There was nobody in sight and the
clouds were wet and low and humid. All around me the world
had grown suddenly very quiet. I could just tell the difference
between the sky and the ocean. And it was all over. I had really
made it! All the way from Oregon. That seemed like years ago.
What if all this never happened? As long as I had kept moving,
the music of the present played on and on. Already that present
was fading into a misty dream. I heard no more music. The faces
of the people I rode with for a day or weeks were receding. I had
stopped only to meet the past.

I did a long exhale and continued to lean against the bike, becoming mesmerized by the lapping water. Lost in reverie, I stared at the calm surface. I wanted to keep the present alive; I wasn't ready for the end. During those minutes I rerode the entire trip as if it were a filmstrip. I saw again the pine forests and great Tetons projected on my mental screen. I felt the snowstorm over Togwotee Pass and relived the indescribable feeling of accomplishment at reaching Hoosier Pass almost 12,000 feet elevation. I watched the red ball of sunrise over Kansas, rode the Missouri roller coaster hills. The eagles I saw in Montana, the hawks of Wyoming, the pair of owls, and the wild flowers of spring were so long ago.

There were a thousand little country stores, but I remembered one in particular. The Sand Lake Grocery surrounded by petunias and pine trees and the coastal beauty of an afternoon in springtime. It was run by a lady who had a look in her eyes I would see time and again all summer. The burning desire to go, too, a longing to be There instead of Here; it didn't matter where, and always that eager, vicarious sharing of your adventure as soon as they would see the loaded bicycle.

As I was leaving, she gave me a postcard with a stamp and her address on it. "Would you mind mailing this back to me when you have completed your trip? I would really like to know that you made it."

She stood in the driveway of her little white frame store in the middle of Oregon's nowhere with beauty and laughter and friendliness all around and watched as I rode away toward — wherever.

I knew that I would make the journey over and over, each time growing better in my mind's eye. I would recall and redefine its unique personality. For this was a journey which I knew from the second day was meant to be. "Nothing went wrong" is an understatement. I didn't even have one flat tire! It was my personal journey whose timing was perfect. I was in all the right places at the right times. With the exception of one hour of rain and one snowstorm, all the days were filled with sunshine and blue skies. Those four hours of misery were just a change of pace. I had tail winds, and the climbs over the mountains seemed to be easier as the summer wore on.

I had shared my summer days with many people and briefly touched hundreds more. I hope I won't forget them too quickly. Yet, I had started out alone and ended alone. How ironic.

"Hey world, I just rode a bicycle across America!" The silent shout echoed and re-echoed in my head and finally came out as a whisper across the gray Atlantic Ocean.

Appendix 2

Sources of Information and Materials

Books and Booklets

Bikecentennial Publications
P.O. Box 8308
Missoula, Montana 59807
(Write to them for a complete list of their publications.)

Delong, Fred, *Delong's Guide to Bicycles and Bicycling*

Coles, Clarence W., and Glenn, Harold T., *Glenn's Complete Bicycle Repair Manual*

Teresi, Dick, *Popular Mechanics Book of Bikes and Bicycling* (New York: Hearst Corporation, 1975).

Thomas, Dian, *Roughing It Easy*

Camping Equipment Suppliers

Eddie Bauer
1737 Airport Way South
Seattle, Washington 98134

L. L. Bean
Freeport, Maine 04033

The North Face
P.O. Box 2399
Station A
Berkeley, California 94702

Recreational Equipment, Inc.
1525 Eleventh Avenue
Seattle, Washington, 98122

Sierra Designs
Fourth and Addison Streets
Berkeley, California 94701

Mail Order Sources for Bicycle Parts

Bikecology Bike Shops
P.O. Box 1880
Santa Monica, California 90406

Cycle Goods Corporation
17701 Leeman Drive
Minnetonka, Minnesota 55343

Cannondale Corp.
35 Pulaski Street
Stamford, Conn. 06902

Palo Alto Bicycle Shop
P.O. Box 1276
Palo Alto, California 94302

The Third Hand
3945 High Street
Eugene, Oregon 97405
(Bicycle tool specialists)

Index